DEFENSE INTELLIGENCE AGENCY

CHINA
MILITARY POWER

MODERNIZING A FORCE *to* FIGHT AND WIN

2019

This report is available online at www.dia.mil/Military-Power-Publications.

For media and public inquiries about this report, contact DIA-PAO@dodiis.mil.

For more information about the Defense Intelligence Agency, visit DIA's website at www.dia.mil.

Information cutoff date, November 2018.

Cover image, Navy frigate *Yantai* of the 11th Chinese naval escort flotilla. Source: Shutterstock.

DIA-02-1706-085

PREFACE

In September 1981, Secretary of Defense Caspar Weinberger asked the Defense Intelligence Agency to produce an unclassified overview of the Soviet Union's military strength. The purpose was to provide America's leaders, the national security community, and the public a comprehensive and accurate view of the threat. The result: the first edition of *Soviet Military Power*. DIA produced over 250,000 copies, and it soon became an annual publication that was translated into eight languages and distributed around the world. In many cases, this report conveyed the scope and breadth of Soviet military strength to U.S. policymakers and the public for the first time.

In the spirit of *Soviet Military Power*, DIA began in 2017 to produce a series of unclassified Defense Intelligence overviews of major foreign military challenges we face. This volume provides details on China's defense and military goals, strategy, plans, and intentions; the organization, structure, and capability of its military supporting those goals; and the enabling infrastructure and industrial base. This product and other reports in the series are intended to inform our public, our leaders, the national security community, and partner nations about the challenges we face in the 21st century.

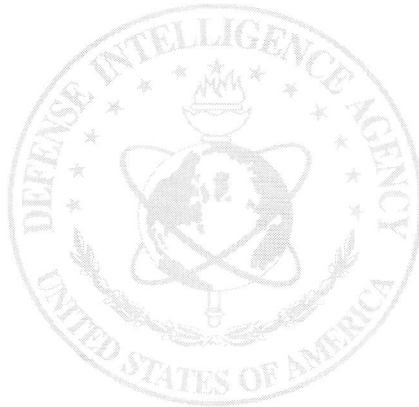

> The 2015 Chinese white paper *China's Military Strategy*, issued by China's State Council Information Office, states: "It is a Chinese Dream to achieve the great rejuvenation of the Chinese nation. The Chinese Dream is to make the country strong....Without a strong military, a country can neither be safe nor strong."

The Defense Intelligence Agency—indeed the broader U.S. Intelligence Community—is continually asked, "What do we need to know about China?" What is China's vision of the world and its role in it? What are Beijing's strategic intentions and what are the implications for Washington? How are the PLA's roles and missions changing as it becomes a more capable military force?

Since Mao Zedong's Communist Revolution in October 1949 brought the Chinese Communist Party to power, China has struggled to identify and align itself with its desired place in the world. Early factional struggles for control of party leadership, decades of negotiations to define territorial boundaries, and continued claims to territories not yet recovered have at times seemed at odds with the self-described nature of the Chinese as peace-loving and oriented only toward their own defense. Chinese leaders historically have been willing to use military force against threats to their regime, whether foreign or domestic, at times preemptively. Lack of significant involvement in military operations during the last several decades has led to a sense of insecurity within the PLA as it seeks to modernize into a great power military.

Still, the United States has at times found itself in direct conflict with China or Chinese forces. China supported two major conflicts in Asia after the Second World War, introducing Chinese volunteer forces in Korea and providing direct Chinese air and air defense support to Hanoi in Vietnam. In addition, China fought border skirmishes with the Soviet Union, India, and a unified Vietnam. In all three cases, military action was an integral part of Chinese diplomatic negotiations. Since then, China has concluded negotiations for most of its land borders (India and Bhutan being the outliers) but remains in contention with Japan, the Philippines, Brunei, Indonesia, Malaysia, and Vietnam over maritime borders, which may in part explain motivation for the PLA Navy's impressive growth and the new emphasis on maritime law enforcement capabilities.

China's double-digit economic growth has slowed recently, but it served to fund several successive defense modernization Five-Year Plans. As international concern over Beijing's human rights policies stymied the PLA's search for ever more sophisticated technologies, China shifted funds and efforts to acquiring technology by any means available. Domestic laws forced foreign partners of Chinese-based joint ventures to release their technology in exchange for entry into China's lucrative market, and China has used other means to secure needed technology and expertise. The result of this multifaceted approach to technology acquisition is a PLA on the verge of fielding some of the most modern weapon systems in the world. In some areas, it already leads the world.

Chinese leaders characterize China's long-term military modernization program as essential to achieving great power status. Indeed, China is building a robust, lethal force with capabilities spanning the air, maritime, space and information domains which will enable China to impose its will in the region. As it continues to grow in strength and confidence, our nation's leaders will face a China insistent on having a greater voice in global interactions, which at times may be antithetical to U.S. interests. With a deeper understanding of the military might behind Chinese economic and diplomatic efforts, we can provide our own national political, economic, and military leaders the widest range of options for choosing when to counter, when to encourage, and when to join with China in actions around the world.

This report offers insights into the modernization of Chinese military power as it reforms from a defensive, inflexible ground-based force charged with domestic and peripheral security responsibilities to a joint, highly agile, expeditionary, and power-projecting arm of Chinese foreign policy that engages in military diplomacy and operations across the globe.

Robert P. Ashley, Jr.
Lieutenant General, U.S. Army
Director
Defense Intelligence Agency

DEFENSE INTELLIGENCE AGENCY

V

CONTENTS

DEFENSE INTELLIGENCE AGENCY

INTENTIONALLY LEFT BLANK

PLA honor guard.

Introduction/Historical Overview

With more than 5,000 years of civilized history, the Chinese nation created a brilliant Chinese civilization, made outstanding contributions to mankind, and became a great nation of the world.

—Chinese President Xi Jinping[1]

China's history dates back nearly five millennia. Historians credit the armies of numerous dynasties throughout those many centuries with unifying the early warring states, building the Great Wall, sending the fleets of early Ming Dynasty maritime explorer Zheng He to far-off foreign lands, and defending against foreign incursions. However, the People's Liberation Army (PLA) has existed for less than a century. Initially referred to as the "Red Army" under Mao Zedong, the PLA is not a national institution but rather the military arm of the Chinese Communist Party (CCP). Established in 1927, the army spent much of its first two decades engaged in fighting the Nationalists led by Chiang Kai-shek during the intermittent Chinese Civil War as well as fighting against the Japanese during World War II (which China refers to as the War of Resistance Against Japan).

Mao's Red Army declared victory over the Nationalists in October 1949, even as combat continued. That same year, the PLA expanded to include the PLA Navy and the PLA Air Force. The PLA remained technologically inferior to Western militaries during its early decades, but China's leaders readily employed PLA forces against the United States in Korea and Vietnam. Beijing's willingness to rely on the PLA as a tool of foreign policy strengthened the PLA's position in China. Even as Mao led China through the upheaval of the Great Leap Forward and the Cultural Revolution, the PLA endured. Although the PLA emerged from the Cultural Revolution in the mid-1970s as one of the stronger pillars of CCP power, its combat power was not commensurate with that of other large states' armed forces.

1978–Present: China's Military Rise

After Deng Xiaoping's assumption of power in 1978, the path to today's PLA was set when national defense was included as the fourth of China's four "modernizations" (the others being industry, science and technology, and agriculture). National defense was accorded the lowest priority, which carried implications for military funding and development. The failure to achieve comprehensive modernization during

Mao's rule was brought home during the 1979 conflict between China and Vietnam, when the PLA's performance exposed grave weaknesses in operational planning, tactics, command and control (C2), logistics, and weaponry. The persistent exchanges of fire with Vietnamese forces during the 1980s highlighted the need for changes even as large numbers of PLA ground troops from around the country were rotated to the border to gain combat experience. Meanwhile, the PLA began to study contemporary foreign, particularly Western, military operations more closely, such as the Falklands War (1982) and the bombing of Libya (1986), for insights on how to modernize China's combat forces.

In 1989, PLA units intervened with lethal force on behalf of the CCP to suppress political demonstrations in Tiananmen Square, which considerably damaged the PLA's domestic and international image. World events in 1991 further shook CCP leaders' confidence in the PLA. The U.S. military's performance in the Persian Gulf War provided the PLA stark lessons regarding the lethal effectiveness of information-enabled weapons and forces, particularly mobility and precision-strike capabilities, that had become the standard for effectively waging war in the modern era. As a result, in the early 1990s Beijing altered its military doctrine, concluding that the most likely conflict that China would face would be a "local war under high-technology conditions" (later amended to "conditions of informatization," referring to warfare in the digital age). This differed markedly from the Mao-era mindset that the PLA would need to be prepared to fight a war more akin to World War II. The PLA's strategy also changed, moving away from the Maoist paradigm of luring an enemy into China to fight a "people's war" with regular troops, irregular (guerrilla) forces, and the general populace. Instead, the PLA began to emphasize a more offensive version of the PLA's historical strategic concept of "active defense": take advantage of longer range, precision-guided munitions (primarily ballistic and cruise missiles) to keep a potential enemy as far as possible from the economically fast-developing Chinese coastal areas by fighting a "noncontact," short, sharp conflict like the Persian Gulf War.

China's changing strategic threat perceptions also shaped military doctrine and the direction of PLA development. Although the Soviet Union had loomed large as a potential military opponent, the threat of a Soviet invasion diminished during the 1980s, shifting the focus away from preparing for a World War II–style conflict. Furthermore, the U.S. 7th Fleet aircraft carrier intervention during the 1996 China-Taiwan "missile crisis" and the accidental NATO strike against China's Embassy in Serbia in 1999 led Beijing to focus on building capabilities to counter U.S. forces in addition to capabilities to dissuade Taiwan from any political activity Beijing deemed unacceptable.

Entering the 21st century, China's leaders recognized the confluence of several factors that led them to expand the scope and quicken the pace of PLA development: China's growing global economic and political interests, rapid technology-driven changes in modern warfare, and perceptions of increased strategic-level external threats, including to China's maritime interests. At this time, Chinese leaders perceived a "period of strategic opportunity" wherein the country presumably would not be involved in a major military conflict before 2020, allowing time for economic and military development. As a result, throughout the late 1990s and early 2000s, China's leaders initiated several practical steps to modernize the PLA as a warfighting instrument.

To accelerate the PLA's modernization and address capability shortfalls, Beijing increased the PLA's budget by an average of 10 percent per year from 2000 to 2016. Beijing also established a PLA General Armaments Department in 1998 to rationalize equipment modernization and acquisition processes, and instituted several broad scientific and technical programs to improve the defense-industrial base and decrease the PLA's dependence on foreign weapon acquisitions. The PLA also revamped its training programs, with all services attempting to prepare more realistically for conflict by emphasizing mission-focused exercises, multiservice operations, mobility, better C2 and staff work, and enhanced logistic support, as well as achieving battlefield advantage by applying "informatized" warfare (regional conflicts defined by real-time, data-networked C2) methods. *[For more on "informatized" warfighting, please see Military Doctrine and Strategy, page 23].*

Beijing also implemented personnel changes to professionalize the PLA. While Beijing was focused on economic development in the late 1970s, the PLA had been allowed to operate nonmilitary businesses to offset limited investment and resources. This led to widespread corruption and drew attention away from training for actual military operations. In 1998, Chinese leaders ordered the PLA to stop operating nonmilitary businesses and focus solely on professional military tasks. As a result, the PLA divested from a number of business ventures but still remains to some extent involved in business schemes. The PLA developed a noncommissioned officer corps and began programs to recruit more technically competent university graduates to operate its modern weapons. PLA political officers assigned to all levels of the military acquired broader personnel management responsibilities in addition to their focus on keeping the PLA ideologically pure and loyal to the CCP.

In 2004, then-President Hu Jintao outlined for the PLA the "Historic Missions of the Armed Forces in the New Period of the New Century," more commonly referred to as the "New Historic Missions of the PLA," to augment the PLA's role as a diplomatic and military instrument and as a guardian of China's global interests. These new missions included ensuring China's sovereignty, territorial integrity, and domestic security; preserving the "period of strategic opportunity" for China's development; safeguarding China's expanding national interests; and helping ensure world peace. Hu's endowment of the PLA with these missions, at a time when economic interests

had become substantial drivers of Beijing's foreign policy, signified a critical inflection point in the PLA's assumption of a global role and transition away from a force bound only to defending China's immediate territorial and sovereignty interests.

Subsequent PLA activities, such as counterpiracy operations in the Gulf of Aden since 2009, international training and exercises, noncombatant evacuations in Libya and Yemen, and expanded peacekeeping operations in Africa under UN auspices, have all been part of China's increasingly ambitious vision for expanding PLA activities to support its growing global clout. China's establishment of its first overseas military base in Djibouti in 2017—overturning Beijing's insistence from its first defense white paper issued in 1998 that China "does not station troops or set up military bases in any foreign country"—is only the latest development in this progression.

The PLA's evolution since President Xi Jinping's transition to power in 2012 has built on the Hu era but also marked a shift, with Xi concurrently taking the helm of the party, military, and state, enabling him to shape the direction of the PLA earlier during his tenure. Xi has focused on strengthening the PLA as a force, underscoring the themes of party rule over the military, improving military capabilities, and enhancing the military's professionalism.[2] Xi has also expanded the scope and ambition of PLA modernization, clearly affirming the PLA's overseas role and providing the institutional framework to enable substantial military growth beyond the PLA's traditional security threats.

PLA troops preparing for parade commemorating the 90th anniversary of the founding of the PLA – September 2017.

Image Source: Shutterstock

In late 2015, President Xi Jinping unveiled the most substantial PLA reforms in at least 30 years. The reforms were designed in part to make the PLA a leaner, more lethal force capable of conducting the types of joint operations that it believes it must master to compete with the U.S. military. Initial reforms established joint theater commands and a new Joint Staff Department while reorganizing the 4 general departments that previously ran the PLA into 15 Central Military Commission (CMC) departments and offices. These efforts aimed to clarify command authorities, integrate China's military services for joint operations, and facilitate Beijing's transition from peace to war.

The structural reforms also established a separate Army headquarters, elevated China's missile force to a full service by establishing the PLA Rocket Force, unified China's space and cyber capabilities under the Strategic Support Force, and created a Joint Logistics Support Force to direct precision support to PLA operations.[3,4,5] The decision to place the Army, which has traditionally played a dominant role in PLA leadership, on equal footing with the PLA's other services underscores a postreform emphasis on jointness. Overall reforms, which the CMC aims to complete by 2020, are expected to touch all levels of the PLA, including cutting approximately 300,000 personnel and refining military doctrine and policies.

[For a more detailed breakdown of PLA services and activities, please see Appendixes A–I.]

In October 2017, China's leaders used the opportunity of its once-in-5-years Party Congress to reduce the size of the CMC, shifting toward a more joint command structure and aligning the military's highest body to its post-reform C2. Reducing the size of the CMC will help Beijing streamline strategic decisionmaking, bolster political oversight of the military, and build a more integrated and professional force. The move also highlights Xi's focus on eliminating corruption, improving party loyalty, and incentivizing operational experience. The CMC now represents a capable and diverse generation of officers with operational experience, which as a whole has the most joint representation in the PLA's history.

In his work report to the 19th Party Congress in October 2017, Xi Jinping called on the PLA to "prepare for military struggle in all strategic directions," and said the military was integral to achieving China's national rejuvenation. In his speech, Xi set three developmental benchmarks for the PLA, including becoming a mechanized force with increased informatized and strategic capabilities by 2020, a fully modernized force by 2035, and a worldwide first-class military by midcentury.[6] The latter two goals build on the call in China's 2013 defense white paper, also issued under Xi, for China's armed forces to achieve a status "commensurate with China's international standing." Viewed in sum, Xi's vision for the PLA constitutes a logical outgrowth of CCP instructions to the PLA since 2004 to protect China's expanding "development interests" at home and abroad.

The extent to which the PLA can progress in its transformation into a world-class military depends on the favorable resolution of several key issues, some of which are longstanding institutional barriers. The PLA's traditional identity as a party army with a military culture that is hierarchical and where decisionmaking is top-down and centralized in some ways is incongruous with efforts to professionalize the PLA and imbue it with a culture that values individual decisionmaking and embraces mission delegation. The PLA also will need to refine newly established C2 structures to enable the execution of dynamic, fast-paced joint military operations and effectively integrate new technologies and processes. Perhaps one of the most difficult challenges of the ongoing reforms is that they represent the institutionalization of a cultural shift within the PLA away from its traditional ground-force-centric, inward-facing model to one that lays the foundation for coequal, professional services capable of joint operations across the globe.

National Military Overview

The People's Liberation Army at a Glance

Services: Army, Navy, Air Force, Rocket Force, Strategic Support Force.

Personnel: Approximately 2 million in regular forces.

Recruit base: Conscription, some volunteer.

Equipment profile: Primarily domestic systems heavily influenced by technology derived from other countries; modern weaponry in each service; some advanced weaponry.

Core strength: Long-range precision strike, information warfare, nuclear retaliatory capability.

Developing strengths: Maritime power projection, special operations.

Key vulnerabilities: Logistics, rigid command structure, joint warfare.

Threat Perceptions

The party's perception that China is facing unprecedented security risks is a driving factor in China's approach to national security.[7] In May 2015, China's State Council Information Office published a white paper titled *China's Military Strategy*, which outlined how Beijing views the global security environment, China's role in that environment, and how the PLA supports that role. The document presented a vision for the PLA's services and emerging security domains that would transform the PLA from its legacy posture to one focused more on long-range mobility. Within the context of Beijing's "period of strategic opportunity," Beijing calculates in *China's Military Strategy* that world war is unlikely

in the immediate future, but China should be prepared for the possibility of local war.

Authoritative Chinese publications typically avoid explicitly listing direct threats, but these threats can be gleaned from several documents that point to Beijing's security concerns.[8] Beijing's primary threat perceptions include sovereignty and domestic security issues that it believes could undermine the overriding strategic objective to perpetuate communist rule. These include longstanding concerns regarding Taiwan independence, Uighur and Tibetan separatism, and perceived challenges to China's control of disputed areas in the East and South China Seas. Authoritative documents also highlight the Korean Peninsula as an area of instability and uncertainty, and express concern regarding unsettled ter-

China's Territorial Claims

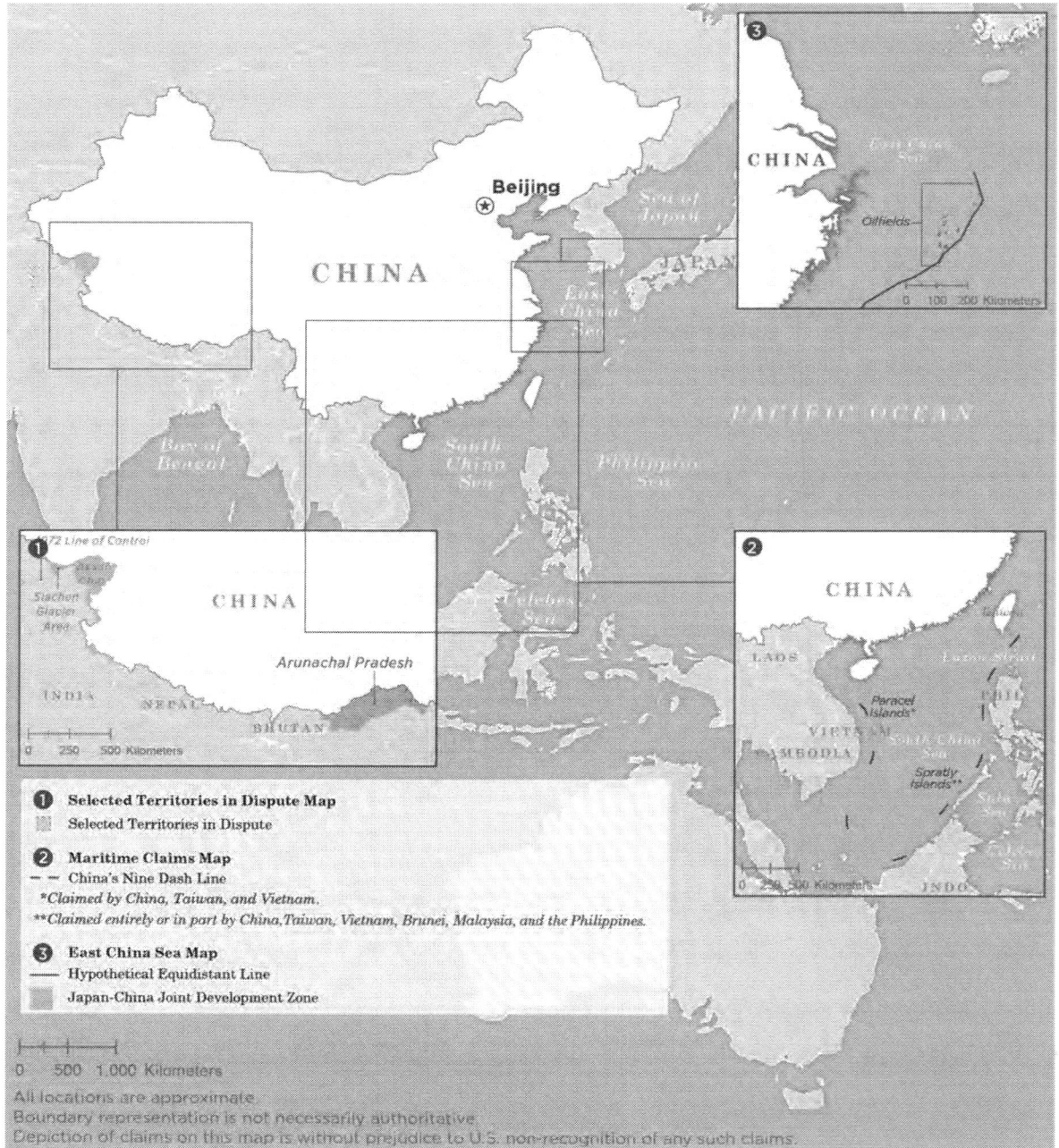

8

ritorial disputes along China's border with India, which periodically result in tense stand-offs like the one that occurred in the summer of 2017 in the disputed Doklam region.[9] Finally, while it calls for a peer-to-peer cooperative relationship with the United States, China also believes that U.S. military presence and U.S.-led security architecture in Asia seeks to constrain China's rise and interfere with China's sovereignty, particularly in a Taiwan conflict scenario and in the East and South China Seas. Since at least the 1990's, Beijing has repeatedly communicated its preference to move away from the U.S.-led regional security system and has pursued its own regional security initiatives in support of what it views as a natural transition to regional predominance.

China's Military Strategy reflects Beijing's drive to establish a coherent, unified approach to managing national security in a world where Beijing perceives that China's expanding interests have made it more vulnerable at home and abroad. The following excerpt from the document illustrates Beijing's perception of this security environment:

In today's world, the global trends toward multipolarity and economic globalization are intensifying, and an information society is rapidly coming into being. Countries are increasingly bound together in a community of shared destiny. Peace, development, cooperation, and mutual benefit have become an irresistible tide of the times.

Profound changes are taking place in the international situation, as manifested in the historic changes in the balance of power, global governance structure, Asia-Pacific geostrategic landscape, and international competition in the economic, scientific and technological, and military fields. The forces for world peace are on the rise; so are the factors against war. In the foreseeable future, a world war is unlikely, and the international situation is expected to remain generally peaceful. There are, however, new threats from hegemonism, power politics, and neointerventionism. International competition for the redistribution of power, rights, and interests is tending to intensify. Terrorist activities are growing increasingly worrisome. Hotspot issues, such as ethnic, religious, border, and territorial disputes, are complex and volatile. Small-scale wars, conflicts, and crises are recurrent in some regions. Therefore, the world still faces both immediate and potential threats of local wars.

—Excerpt from *China's Military Strategy*, May 2015

China's Military Strategy is directed primarily at an internal audience. Thus, it is replete with party jargon, but it does contain the broad underpinnings of China's military decision-making calculus. For example, Beijing sees both threats and opportunities emerging from the evolution of the international community beyond the U.S.-led unipolar framework toward a more integrated global environment shaped by major-power dynamics. Furthermore, China sees itself as an emerging major power that will be able to gain influence as long as it can maintain a stable periphery. As it emerges, Beijing will use its growing power to shape the regional environment in the face of interconnected threats while trying to avoid conflict over core interests: sovereignty, development, and unification. More specifically, China believes it must plan to address the many threats to regional stability because they are individually complex and at the same time contain a potential for external actors, most importantly the United States, to become involved. Nevertheless, China must also look to safeguard its international interests as they multiply and incur additional threats. Finally, as new threats emerge and as other militaries adjust their acquisition, strategies, and structure, China knows the PLA must be prepared to fight in new realms and adapt to the modern, high-tech battlefield.

With a generally favorable external environment, China will remain in an important period of strategic opportunities for its development, a period in which much can be achieved. China's comprehensive national strength, core competitiveness and risk-resistance capacity are notably increasing, and China enjoys growing international standing and influence. Domestically, the Chinese people's standard of living has remarkably improved, and Chinese society remains stable. China, as a large developing country, still faces multiple and complex security threats, as well as increasing external impediments and challenges. Subsistence and development security concerns, as well as traditional and nontraditional security threats, are interwoven. Therefore, China has an arduous task to safeguard its national unification, territorial integrity and development interests.

As the world economic and strategic center of gravity is shifting ever more rapidly to the Asia-Pacific region, the U.S. carries on its 'rebalancing' strategy and enhances its military presence and its military alliances in this region. Japan is sparing no effort to dodge the postwar mechanism, overhauling its military and security policies. Such development has caused grave concerns among other countries in the region. On the issues concerning China's territorial sovereignty and maritime rights and interests, some of its offshore neighbors take provocative actions and reinforce their military presence on China's reefs and islands that they have illegally occupied. Some external countries are also busy meddling in South China Sea affairs; a tiny few maintain constant close-in air and sea surveillance and reconnaissance against China. It is thus a longstanding task for China to safeguard its maritime rights and interests. Certain disputes over land territory are still smoldering. The Korean Peninsula and Northeast Asia are shrouded in instability and uncertainty. Regional terrorism, separatism, and extremism are rampant. All these have a negative impact on the security and stability along China's periphery.

The Taiwan issue bears on China's reunification and long-term development, and reunification is an inevitable trend in the course of national rejuvenation. In recent years, cross–Taiwan Strait relations have sustained a sound momentum of peaceful development, but the root cause of instability has not yet been removed, and the 'Taiwan independence' separatist forces and their activities are still the biggest threat to the peaceful development of cross-strait relations. Further, China faces a formidable task to maintain political security and social stability. Separatist forces for 'East Turkistan independence' and 'Tibet independence' have inflicted serious damage, particularly with escalating violent terrorist activities by East Turkistan independence forces. Besides, anti-China forces have never given up their attempt to instigate a 'color revolution' in this country. Consequently, China faces more challenges in terms of national security and social stability. With the growth of China's national interests, its national security is more vulnerable to international and regional turmoil, terrorism, piracy, serious natural disasters, and epidemics, and the security of overseas interests concerning energy and resources, strategic sea lines of communication (SLOCs), as well as institutions, personnel, and assets abroad, has become an imminent issue.

The world revolution in military affairs (RMA) is proceeding to a new stage. Long-range, precise, smart, stealthy, and unmanned weapons and equipment are becoming increasingly sophisticated. Outer space and cyberspace have become new commanding heights in strategic competition among all parties. The form of war is accelerating its evolution to informatization. World major powers are actively adjusting their national security strategies and defense policies and speeding up their military transformation and force restructuring. The aforementioned revolutionary changes in military technologies and the form of war have not only had a significant impact on the international political and military landscapes but also posed new and severe challenges to China's military security.

—Excerpt from *China's Military Strategy*, May 2015

National Security Strategy

Making progress while maintaining stability.

—Xi Jinping in his address to the 19th Party Congress[10]

China's leaders see China as a country that is "moving closer to center stage" to achieve the "great rejuvenation of the Chinese nation."[11] This ambition permeates China's national security strategy and the PLA's role in supporting the party. Since the early 1980s, when China initiated its Reform and Opening policy, China's economy has grown rapidly. The CCP remained focused primarily on economic growth throughout the 1980s and 1990s, and in the early 2000s it identified the initial decades of the 21st century as a "period of strategic opportunity" in the international environment that would allow China to focus on building "comprehensive national power." The CCP's contemporary strategic objectives are to:

- Perpetuate CCP rule.

- Maintain domestic stability.

- Sustain economic growth and development.

- Defend national sovereignty and territorial integrity.

- Secure China's status as a great power.

China has taken deliberate steps to modernize the CCP, its military, the government, and other institutions in an attempt to improve coherence. Before 2015, departments across the government formulated separate security strategies, but in early 2015, China's leaders adopted China's first publicly released national security strategy outline, a framework to guide China's approach to addressing both domestic and international security threats, and called for international engagement to address shared security problems.[12]

The strategy outlines Beijing's aim to ensure security, promote modernization, as well as preserve China's socialist system. In addition to the strategic objectives above, the document emphasized the necessity of contributing to world peace and development and called for attention to promoting "rule of law" in support of national security.[13] This led the National People's Congress to pass a package of laws in 2015 and 2016 intended to address national security concerns, including harsher punishments for crimes involving terrorism and extremism, cybersecurity measures, and increased restrictions for foreign nongovernmental organizations.[14,15]

Although China's national security strategy outline contained both inward- and outward-looking elements, Beijing's view of China's role in the international community was further elaborated in an article on Xi Jinping's thoughts on diplomacy published in mid-2017 by one of

China's top diplomats, Yang Jiechi. Yang paints a picture of Chinese diplomacy that focuses on China's ambition for national rejuvenation and becoming a world power. Yang describes a confident China that is ready to "shoulder its responsibility as a major country" and build a global network of partnerships, but one that is resolved and uncompromising as it upholds its sovereignty and security interests.[16]

The PLA's Role in National Security

China's Military Strategy built on a series of biennial defense reviews that Beijing published beginning in 1998 to mitigate international concern about the lack of transparency of its military modernization. What differentiated the document from its predecessors was that it, for the first time, publicly clarified the PLA's role in protecting China's evolving national security interests and shed light on policies, such as the PLA's commitment to nuclear deterrence. The report affirmed many of China's longstanding defense policies but also signaled a shift toward emerging security domains, such as cyber and space, and also emphasized the need to focus on global maritime operations.

The report outlined eight "strategic tasks," or types of missions the PLA must be ready to execute:[17]

- Safeguard the sovereignty of China's territory.

- Safeguard national unification.

- Safeguard China's interests in new domains, such as space and cyberspace.

- Safeguard China's overseas interests.

- Maintain strategic deterrence.

- Participate in international security cooperation.

- Maintain China's political security and social stability.

- Conduct emergency rescue, disaster relief, and "rights and interest protection" missions.

Beijing almost certainly views these missions as necessary national security tasks for China to claim great-power status. In 2017, Beijing emphasized several of these tasks in its "White Paper on China's Policies on Asia Pacific Security Cooperation," stressing the need for a PLA that is able to conduct expeditionary operations and other activities to defend and secure growing Chinese national interests overseas from "destabilizing and uncertain factors."[18] The PLA coordinates with China's law enforcement, Foreign Ministry, and other security entities as needed on military-related activities, particularly operations beyond China's borders.

Military Leadership

China's military leaders are influential in defense and foreign policy. As the CCP's armed wing, the PLA is organizationally part of the party apparatus. Career military officers for the most part are party members, and units at the company level and above have political officers responsible for personnel decisions, propaganda, and counterintelligence. These political officers also are responsible for ensuring that party orders are carried out throughout the PLA. CCP committees, led by the political officers and military commanders, make major decisions in units at all levels.[19]

The CMC, the PLA's highest decisionmaking body, is technically both a party organ subordinate to the CCP Central Committee and a governmental office appointed by the National People's Congress, but it is staffed almost exclusively by military officers. The CMC chairman is a civilian who usually serves concurrently as the CCP general secretary and China's president. During the past decade, the CMC's membership has included two military vice chairmen who serve concurrently on the politburo; the minister of national defense, who serves as the face of the military for foreign engagement; the service commanders; and the directors of the four general headquarters departments. This framework occasionally shifts; it was revised during the 19th Party Congress in October 2017, at which

Xi Jinping, CCP General Secretary, President and Central Military Commission Chairman.

point the service chiefs were removed from the body, leaving the chairman, vice chairmen, minister of national defense, Joint Staff Department chief, Political Work Department director, and Discipline Inspection Commission secretary.[20,21] These changes align the military's top body to its postreform structure and underscore key themes of jointness, party loyalty, and anticorruption.

People's Liberation Army's Organizational Structure [22,23]

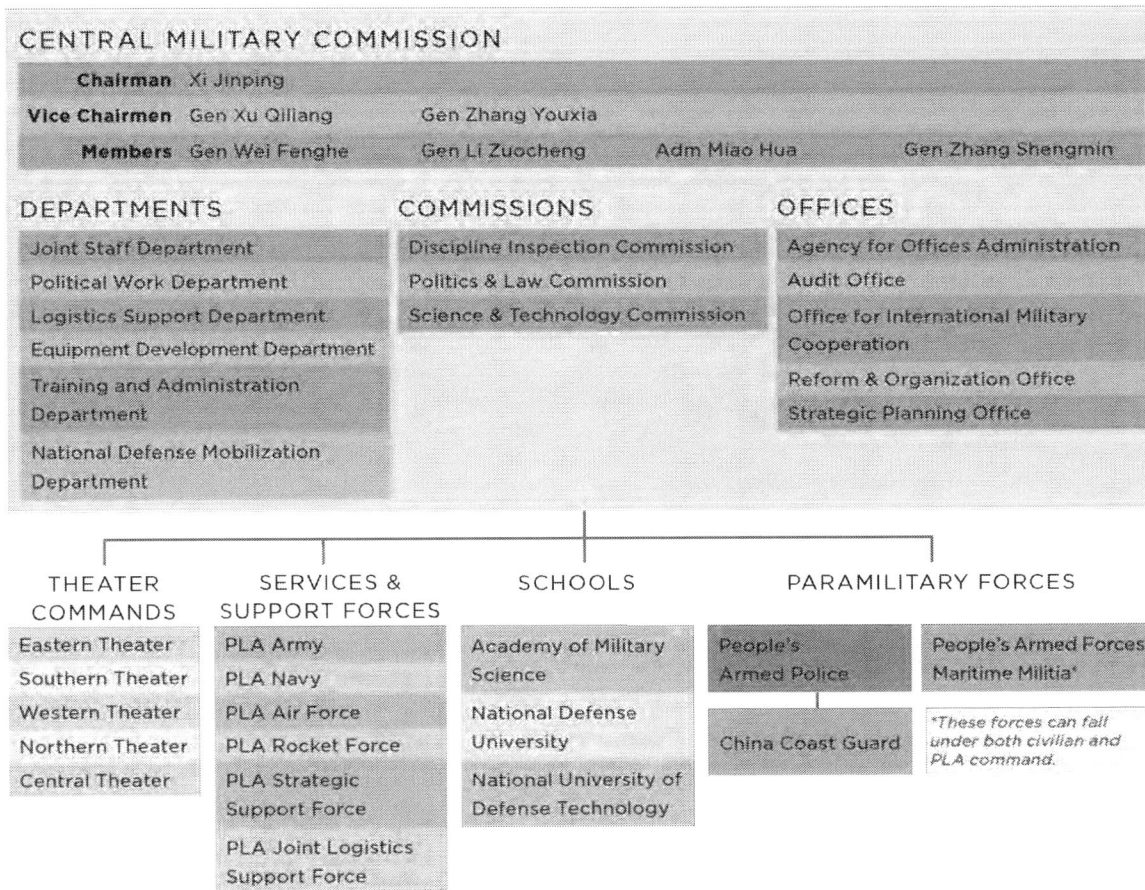

CENTRAL MILITARY COMMISSION

Chairman	Xi Jinping			
Vice Chairmen	Gen Xu Qiliang	Gen Zhang Youxia		
Members	Gen Wei Fenghe	Gen Li Zuocheng	Adm Miao Hua	Gen Zhang Shengmin

DEPARTMENTS	COMMISSIONS	OFFICES
Joint Staff Department	Discipline Inspection Commission	Agency for Offices Administration
Political Work Department	Politics & Law Commission	Audit Office
Logistics Support Department	Science & Technology Commission	Office for International Military Cooperation
Equipment Development Department		
Training and Administration Department		Reform & Organization Office
National Defense Mobilization Department		Strategic Planning Office

THEATER COMMANDS	SERVICES & SUPPORT FORCES	SCHOOLS	PARAMILITARY FORCES	
Eastern Theater	PLA Army	Academy of Military Science	People's Armed Police	People's Armed Forces Maritime Militia*
Southern Theater	PLA Navy			
Western Theater	PLA Air Force	National Defense University	China Coast Guard	*These forces can fall under both civilian and PLA command.
Northern Theater	PLA Rocket Force			
Central Theater	PLA Strategic Support Force	National University of Defense Technology		
	PLA Joint Logistics Support Force			

Image Source: DIA, D5 Design

Ministry of National Defense and general offices are not depicted in this chart.

Political Work in the PLA

The PLA has been a politicized "party army" since its inception and exists to guarantee the CCP regime's survival above all else, serving the state as a secondary role, in contrast to most Western militaries, which are considered apolitical, professional forces that first and foremost serve the state.

Maintaining this party-military identity even as the PLA embarks on major structural reforms is the top priority for China's leadership. PLA reforms include establishment of the Political Work Department, which appears to have assumed many responsibilities of the former General Political Department. The PLA's political work system is the primary means through which the CCP "controls the gun" in accordance with Mao Zedong's famous dictum that "political power grows out of the barrel of a gun." Most PLA officers are party members, and in recent decades, PLA officers typically have constituted about 20 percent of the CCP's Central Committee. Moreover, since 1997 the two uniformed vice chairmen of the CMC have served concurrently on the CCP Politburo.

- The tiers of political work in the PLA are interlocking, reinforcing systems that allow the CCP to penetrate the military from top to bottom. These tiers comprise the political commissar system, the party committee system, and the party discipline inspection system.

- Political commissars are responsible for personnel, education, security, discipline, and morale. The Political Work Department, the director of which serves on the CMC, manages the PLA's political commissars and is the locus for day-to-day political work in the military.

- The party committee system is replicated in some fashion at each level of command. Party committees fall under the supervision of the CMC Political Work Department and are intended to ensure loyalty at all levels. They propagate the party positions, policies, and directives throughout the force.

- Party discipline inspection bodies monitor the performance of party members in the military and ensure "upright" behavior. The PLA Central Discipline Inspection Commission (CDIC) was elevated to the CMC level during recent restructuring from its previous position as a subordinate office within the former General Political Department.[24] These changes culminated with the CDIC head's appointment as a member of the CMC during the 19th Party Congress. The CDIC has played a key role within the military in recent years, overseeing investigations to weed out graft and uproot politically powerful networks in the ranks as part of China's ongoing anticorruption campaign. In November 2015, Xi also announced the creation of a new PLA Politics and Law Commission, mirroring a similar party organization that oversees legal and judicial issues in the state bureaucracy.[25]

Stability Issues

> We must do more to safeguard China's sovereignty, security, and development interests, and staunchly oppose all attempts to split China or undermine its ethnic unity and social harmony and stability.
>
> —Xi Jinping, speech at the 19th Party Congress

China's leaders for decades have prioritized domestic stability and the continued rule of the CCP. Since the 1990s, however, China has confronted chronic social protest spurred by an often unresponsive and corrupt political and legal system, and a range of economic, social, and environmental problems. Under President Xi Jinping, Beijing has responded to these challenges with a mixture of increased repression and CCP-led efforts to address some of these underlying problems. Xi is using the CCP to assert control over all facets of the Chinese state, restricting the space for independent activity across social, political, and economic spheres.

People's Armed Police in formation during antiterrorism drill for the 2008 Beijing Olympics.

DEFENSE INTELLIGENCE AGENCY

This push includes a sweeping anticorruption campaign, a faithfully propagandistic media, a tightly constrained civil society, and an all-encompassing concept of national security.[26]

In ethnic minority regions such as Tibet and Xinjiang, the CCP has promulgated repressive regulations against alleged extremism by tightening limits on peaceful religious expression and ethnic identity. Beginning in April 2017, Xinjiang authorities detained hundreds of thousands, possibly millions, of Muslims in the region ostensibly for antiextremism reeducation. As part of the Xinjiang campaign, security officials greatly expanded their use of high-tech and big-data surveillance systems, which they are expected to extend countrywide in an effort to curb social unrest.[27]

China's armed forces support the CCP's domestic ambitions without question. In 2015, top military guidance reaffirmed this role as one of the force's main strategic tasks: "maintain China's political security and social stability."[28] China's military and paramilitary leaders are actively developing doctrine and forces to backstop local police, respond to riots and natural disasters, and stop terrorism.

The People's Armed Police (PAP) is at the forefront of this mission. The PAP is a paramilitary force of more than 500,000 troops that for decades has focused on domestic security and economic development tasks under the shared command of the CMC and State Council. In 2018, Beijing moved the PAP entirely under CMC control and out of civilian channels, and announced additional reforms intended to modernize its force structure, streamline its command system, and increase its operational effectiveness.[29] Changes to the PAP also reflect a shift toward a more operational mindset, trading legacy site-security missions for rapid-deployment counterterrorism and maritime patrols.[30]

In recent years, Beijing's longstanding suspicion that so-called "hostile foreign influences" constitute a significant threat to internal stability and CCP rule has led it to step up efforts to pursue political security-related goals overseas. In 2015, China passed a counterterrorism law that included a provision authorizing PLA, PAP, police, and intelligence operations abroad—evidence that party leaders are considering this possibility.[31]

External Defense Relations

In the spirit of neighborhood diplomacy of friendship, sincerity, reciprocity, and inclusiveness, China's armed forces will further develop relations with their counterparts in neighboring countries. Also, they will work to raise the level of military relations with European counterparts [and] continue the traditional friendly military ties with their African, Latin American, and Southern Pacific counterparts. China's armed forces will work to further defense and security cooperation in the Shanghai Cooperation Organization and continue to participate in multilateral dialogues and cooperation mechanisms, such as the Association of Southeast Asian Nations (ASEAN) Defense Ministers' Meeting Plus, ASEAN Regional Forum, Shangri-La Dialogue, Jakarta International Defence Dialogue, and Western Pacific Naval Symposium. The Chinese military will continue to host multilateral events like the Xiangshan Forum, striving to establish a new framework for security and cooperation conducive to peace, stability, and prosperity in the Asia-Pacific region.

—Excerpt from *China's Military Strategy*, May 2015

The PLA engages with foreign militaries to demonstrate its growing capabilities; improve its tactics, techniques, and procedures; enhance China's image and influence abroad, and further China's diplomatic objectives. Bilateral and multilateral exercises provide political benefits to China and opportunities for the PLA to improve capabilities in areas such as counterterrorism, mobility operations, and logistics. Senior-level visits and exchanges provide China with opportunities to increase military officers' international exposure, communicate China's positions to foreign audiences, understand alternative worldviews, and advance foreign relations through interpersonal contacts and military assistance programs.

China advances its day-to-day overseas military diplomacy using PLA officers assigned as military attachés in at least 110 countries.[32]

China's military attachés serve as military advisers to the ambassador, support Ministry of Foreign Affairs and PLA foreign policy objectives, and perform a variety of duties tied to PLA military and security cooperation, including counterpart exchanges with host nation and third-country personnel. Expanded PLA travel abroad enables PLA officers to observe and study foreign military command structures, unit formations, and operational training.[33]

As China's regional and international interests have grown, the PLA has substantially expanded its international engagement, especially in the areas of peacekeeping operations (PKOs), counterpiracy, humanitarian assistance and disaster relief (HADR), counterterrorism, and multinational combined exercises. For example, many Latin American and Caribbean countries send officers to

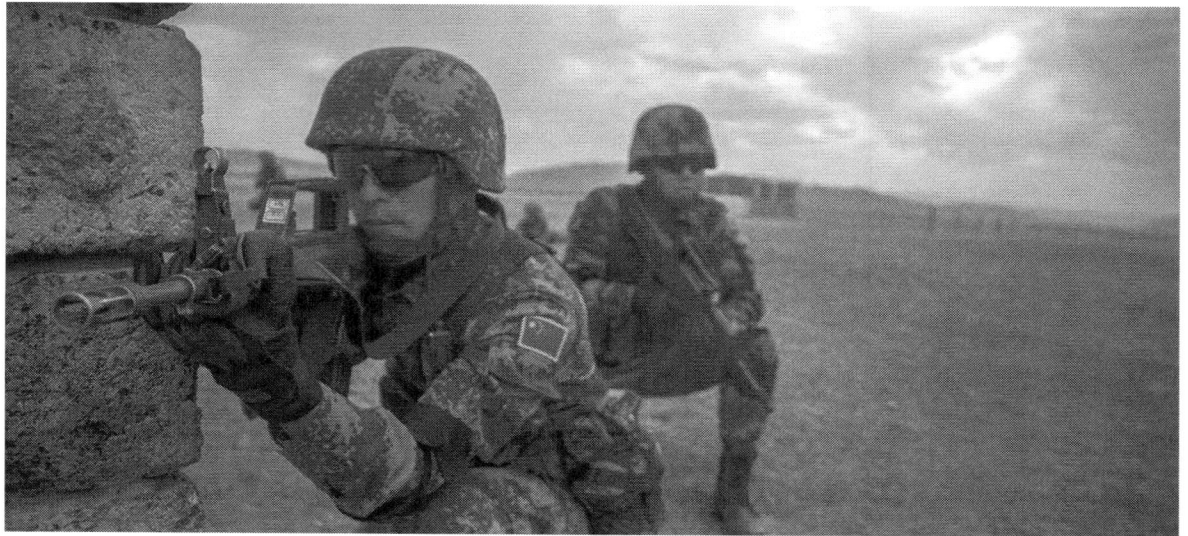

PLA soldiers conduct individual movement training.

the strategic-level College of Defense Studies at China's National Defense University; some of these countries also send officers to other PLA schools. In addition to furthering PLA modernization, these engagements probably will remain focused on building China's political ties, explaining China's rise, and building China's international influence, particularly in Asia, Africa, and Latin America.[34]

Defense Budget

China's approach to funding security requirements has been deliberate and substantial. China's military spending increased by an average of 10 percent (inflation adjusted) per year from 2000 to 2016 and has gradually slowed to 5- to 7-percent growth during the past 2 years. The official defense budget has remained at 1.2 to 1.4 percent of gross domestic product for the past decade, allowing for steady, sustainable expenditure growth and qualitative improvements throughout the PLA.

Estimating actual military expenses is difficult because of China's poor accounting transparency and incomplete transition to a market economy. The formal defense budget process does not include funding for foreign weapons procurement, some research and development (R&D), and certain personnel benefits. Other government ministries distribute defense funds in addition to extrabudgetary funds that supplement personnel living subsidies, equipment maintenance, and other budgetary items.[35,36]

However, using 2018 prices and exchange rates as an example, China's total military-related spending for 2018 probably exceeded $200 billion, a threefold increase since 2002. Such spending has been on the rise since the 1990s, when China formally began to emphasize defense-related programs throughout the course of several "Five-Year Plans."

Although the total dollar value of China's defense budget remains significantly below that of the United States, China has benefited from "latecomer advantage." In other words, China has not had to invest in costly R&D of new technologies to the same degree as the United States. Rather, China has routinely adopted the best and most effective platforms found in foreign militaries through direct purchase, retrofits, or theft of intellectual property. By doing so, China has been able to focus on expediting its military modernization at a small fraction of the original cost.

China's Official Defense Spending 2007-2018 (billions of 2018 dollars)

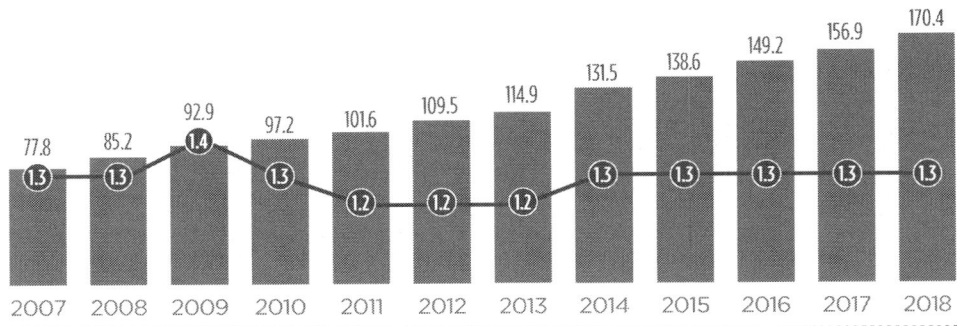

Year	2007	2008	2009	2010	2011	2012	2013	2014	2015	2016	2017	2018
Real defense expenditures	77.8	85.2	92.9	97.2	101.6	109.5	114.9	131.5	138.6	149.2	156.9	170.4
% of GDP	1.3	1.3	1.4	1.3	1.2	1.2	1.2	1.3	1.3	1.3	1.3	1.3

■ Real defense expenditures (Billions 2018 USD, Adjusted for Inflation)

—●— % of GDP

DEFENSE INTELLIGENCE AGENCY

Image Source: DIMOC

Jiangkai II class frigate *Hengshui* conducting gunnery exercise.

Military Doctrine and Strategy

China's military goal is to build a strong, combat-effective force capable of winning regional conflicts and employing integrated, real-time C2 networks.[37] The doctrine that supports this strategy is evolving with ongoing PLA reforms. For instance, in 2017 the PLA began to implement revised military training regulations that focused on realistic training for modern warfare and preparations for joint combat operations.[38]

China characterizes its military strategy as one of "active defense," a concept it describes as strategically defensive but operationally offensive. The strategy is rooted in the concept that once Beijing has determined that an adversary has damaged or intends to damage China's interests at the strategic level, Beijing will be justified in responding "defensively" at the operational or tactical level, even if the adversary has not yet conducted offensive military operations. Beijing interprets active defense to include mandates for deescalating a conflict and seizing the initiative during a conflict, and has enshrined the concept in China's National Security Law (2015) and in the PLA's major strategy documents.[39] President Xi's speech during the 90th anniversary parade of the PLA further highlighted that China would never conduct "invasion and expansion" but would never permit "any piece of Chinese territory" to separate from China.[40]

China's approach to its dispute with Japan over the Senkaku Islands partially illustrates this concept: China has employed both military and law enforcement assets proactively to challenge Japan's administration of the islands since Beijing determined that Japan's purchase of the islands from a private owner in 2012 constituted a serious infringement on China's sovereignty claims. Although the PLA has not yet carried out kinetic strikes on Japanese forces around the islands, China's active defense concept could potentially justify such attacks if Beijing perceived Japan to have further escalated the dispute.

Perceptions of Modern Conflict

The PLA often uses the term "informatization" to describe the transformation process of becoming a modern military that can operate in the digital age. The concept figures prominently in PLA writings and is roughly analogous to the U.S. military's concept of net-centric capability: a force's ability to use advanced information technology and communications systems to gain operational advantage over an adversary. The PLA uses the term "informatized warfare" to describe the process of acquiring, transmitting, processing, and using information to conduct joint military operations across the domains of land, sea, air, space, cyberspace, and the electromagnetic spectrum during a conflict. PLA writings highlight the benefit of near-real-time shared awareness of the battlefield in enabling quick, unified effort to seize tactical opportunities.[41]

In 2015, China's leaders adjusted guidance on the type of war the PLA should be prepared to fight by directing the PLA to be capable of fighting and winning "informatized local wars," with an emphasis on "maritime military struggle." Chinese military strategy documents also emphasize the growing importance of offensive air operations, long-distance mobility operations, and space and cyber operations. In other words, China expects that its future wars mostly will be fought outside its borders and will involve conflict in the maritime domain. China promulgated this through its most recent update to its "military strategic guidelines," the top-level directives that China's leaders use to define concepts, assess threats, and set priorities for planning, force posture, and modernization.[42]

The PLA considers information the critical enabler for these maritime-focused digital-age operations, and as a result, China invests heavily in the development and proliferation of intelligence, surveillance, and reconnaissance equipment, force structure, and a universal network that processes information across all of its operational domains. These domains include C2, comprehensive support, multidimensional protection, joint firepower strike, and battlefield maneuver.

National Military Command and Control

A key driver of ongoing military reforms is Beijing's desire to increase the PLA's ability to carry out joint operations on a modern, high-tech battlefield.[43] Prior to reforms, no permanent joint C2 mechanism existed. In fact, service headquarters had operational authority over their own forces during peacetime, and the former Army-centric military regions were responsible for conducting joint operations during wartime, although this was never attempted. This construct was impractical because it would have forced the PLA to transition from a service-oriented peacetime construct to a war-ready joint construct on a moment's notice. Senior leaders recognized this flaw, and President Xi remarked in 2013 that "establishing a joint C2 system should be given primary importance, and establishing a CMC and theater command joint C2 system should not be delayed."[44]

Consequently, core elements of national- and regional-level military reforms since 2015 have focused on refining the PLA's C2 structure, producing a joint operational command system with decisionmaking emanating from the CMC to theater commands and down to operational units.[45,46] The reform plan aimed to establish two clear lines of authority under the CMC, giving the services authority over force management issues while empowering theater headquarters to command operations—a distinction that had been ambiguous.[47] One aspect of the new structure that is different from previous Chinese military C2 is the permanence of operational C2, which eliminates the need to create ad hoc wartime commands. This system theoretically gives China the ability to quickly transition to a war footing. Speaking on behalf of the PLA, a Ministry of National Defense spokesman said reforms sought to improve "leadership administration and command of joint operations" so that the PLA would have a force structure able to fight and win modern conflicts.

Core Elements of Command and Control Reform

Theater Commands. The PLA transitioned from seven military regions to five "theaters of operations," or joint commands.[48] This structure is aligned toward Beijing's perceived "strategic directions," geographic areas of strategic importance along China's periphery in which the PLA must be prepared to operate.

Joint Operations Command Centers. The cornerstone of the military's new joint C2 system is the PLA's national- and theater-level joint operations command centers (JOCCs), staffed by personnel drawn from all services. The national-level joint operations command center, also known as the CMC JOCC, coordinates the efforts of the five theater commands to achieve the PLA's strategic objectives. The theater-level JOCCs are responsible for all tasks in their area of responsibility, including carrying out around-the-clock watch functions, maintaining situational awareness, managing joint exercises, and providing a communications hub linking theater commanders with service component commanders and forces.[49]

According to China's Ministry of National Defense, the Theater of Operations construct will enhance combat effectiveness.

Joint Staff Department. During PLA reforms, the CMC dissolved the former General Staff Department, establishing a number of CMC-subordinate departments from the former organization. According to the Ministry of National Defense, the Joint Staff Department (JSD) is responsible for combat planning, C2 support, and formulating strategy and requirements.[50] The formation of the CMC JSD is likely to result in more streamlined and efficient operational planning because other former General Staff Department functions, such as mobilization, training, and administration, have been assumed by separate departments. The JSD is purported to have greater representation from across the PLA's services, potentially enhancing joint operational planning and execution.[51]

Modernizing Joint Command and Control

China continues to place a high priority on modernizing the PLA's command, control, communications, computers, intelligence, surveillance, and reconnaissance (C4ISR) system as a response to trends in modern warfare that emphasize the importance of rapid decisionmaking and information sharing and processing. The PLA is seeking to improve its technological capabilities and organizational structure to command complex joint operations in near and distant battlefields with increasingly sophisticated weapons.[52]

Supporting the reforms with technological improvements to C4ISR systems is essential to improving the speed and effectiveness of decisionmaking while providing secure, reliable communications to fixed and mobile command posts. The PLA is fielding advanced automated command systems, such as its Integrated Command Platform, with units at lower echelons across the force. The adoption of the Integrated Command Platform enables multiservice communications necessary for joint operations.

> In the implementation of the military strategic guideline in the new situation, China's armed forces must closely center around the CPC's [Communist Party's] goal of building a strong military, respond to the state's core security needs, aim at building an informatized military and winning informatized wars, deepen the reform of national defense and the armed forces in an all-round way, build a modern system of military forces with Chinese characteristics, and constantly enhance their capabilities for addressing various security threats and accomplishing diversified military tasks.
>
> —Excerpt from *China's Military Strategy*, May 2015

New technologies which are being introduced into the PLA enable sharing of information—intelligence, battlefield information, logistic information, and weather reports—on robust, redundant communication networks to improve commanders' situational awareness. In particular, the transmission of intelligence, surveillance, and reconnaissance (ISR) data in near-real time to commanders in the field could facilitate the commanders' decisionmaking processes and make operations more efficient.[53]

As these technical improvements are brought on line, they greatly enhance the PLA's flexibility and responsiveness. Informatized operations no longer require in-person meetings for command decisionmaking or labor-intensive processes for execution. Commanders can issue orders to multiple units at the same time while on the move, and units can rapidly adjust their actions through the use of digital databases and command automation tools.

The nature of these reform and modernization efforts in part resembles a Western-style joint C2 structure in which operational commanders develop force packages from units that are trained and equipped by the services. The creation of a permanent joint C2 structure that places more emphasis on naval and aerospace forces, along with a dedicated Strategic Support Force responsible for electronic warfare and operations in the space and cyberspace domains, reflects an emerging PLA capacity to more effectively execute joint operations.[54]

PLA Navy sailors manning an Integrated Command Platform command post.

Regional and Global Operations

Even as PLA capabilities have improved and units have begun to operate farther from the Chinese mainland, Beijing has continued to emphasize what it perceives as a "period of strategic opportunity" during which it can pursue development without a major military conflict. In line with this perception, Beijing has implemented an approach to external engagement that seeks to enhance China's reach and power through activities calculated to fall below the threshold of alarming the international community about China's rise or provoking the United States, its allies and partners, or others in the Asia-Pacific region into military conflict or an anti-China coalition. This is particularly evident in China's pursuit of its territorial and maritime sovereignty claims in the South and East China Seas. In the South China Sea, China primarily uses maritime law enforcement ships, with its Navy ships in protective positions, to pressure other claimants and limit access to Chinese-occupied features. China's expansion of disputed features and construction in the Spratly Islands using large-scale land reclamation demonstrates China's capacity—and a shift in willingness to exercise that capacity short of military conflict—to strengthen China's control over disputed areas, enhance China's presence, and challenge other claimants.[55]

Luhai class destroyer *Shenzhen.*

Image Source: DIMOC

China's maritime emphasis and concern with protecting its overseas interests have increasingly drawn the PLA beyond China's borders and immediate periphery. The evolving focus of the PLA Navy (PLAN)—from "offshore waters defense" to a mix of offshore waters defense and "open-seas protection"—reflects China's desire for a wider operational reach. Since 2009, the PLA has incrementally expanded its global operations beyond the previously limited port calls and UN PKO missions. The PLAN has expanded the scope and frequency of extended-range naval deployments, military exercises, and engagements.

The establishment in Djibouti of the PLA's first overseas military base with a deployed company of Marines and equipment, and probable follow-on bases at other locations, signals a turning point in the expansion of PLA operations in the Indian Ocean region and beyond.[56,57,58,59] These bases, and other improvements to the PLA's ability to project power during the next decade, will increase China's ability to deter by military force and sustain operations abroad.

DEFENSE INTELLIGENCE AGENCY

29

PLAN helicopter operating near the Jiangkai II class *Hengshui.*

Core Chinese Military Capabilities

Whereas the PLA of Mao's era was ground-force-centric and lacked most modern capabilities such as mechanized troop transportation, investments in modernization have expanded China's military capabilities across all warfare domains.

Today's PLA is still far from being able to deploy large numbers of conventional forces globally, but China has developed nuclear, space, cyberspace, and other capabilities that can reach potential adversaries across the globe.

DEFENSE INTELLIGENCE AGENCY

31

The First and Second Island Chains

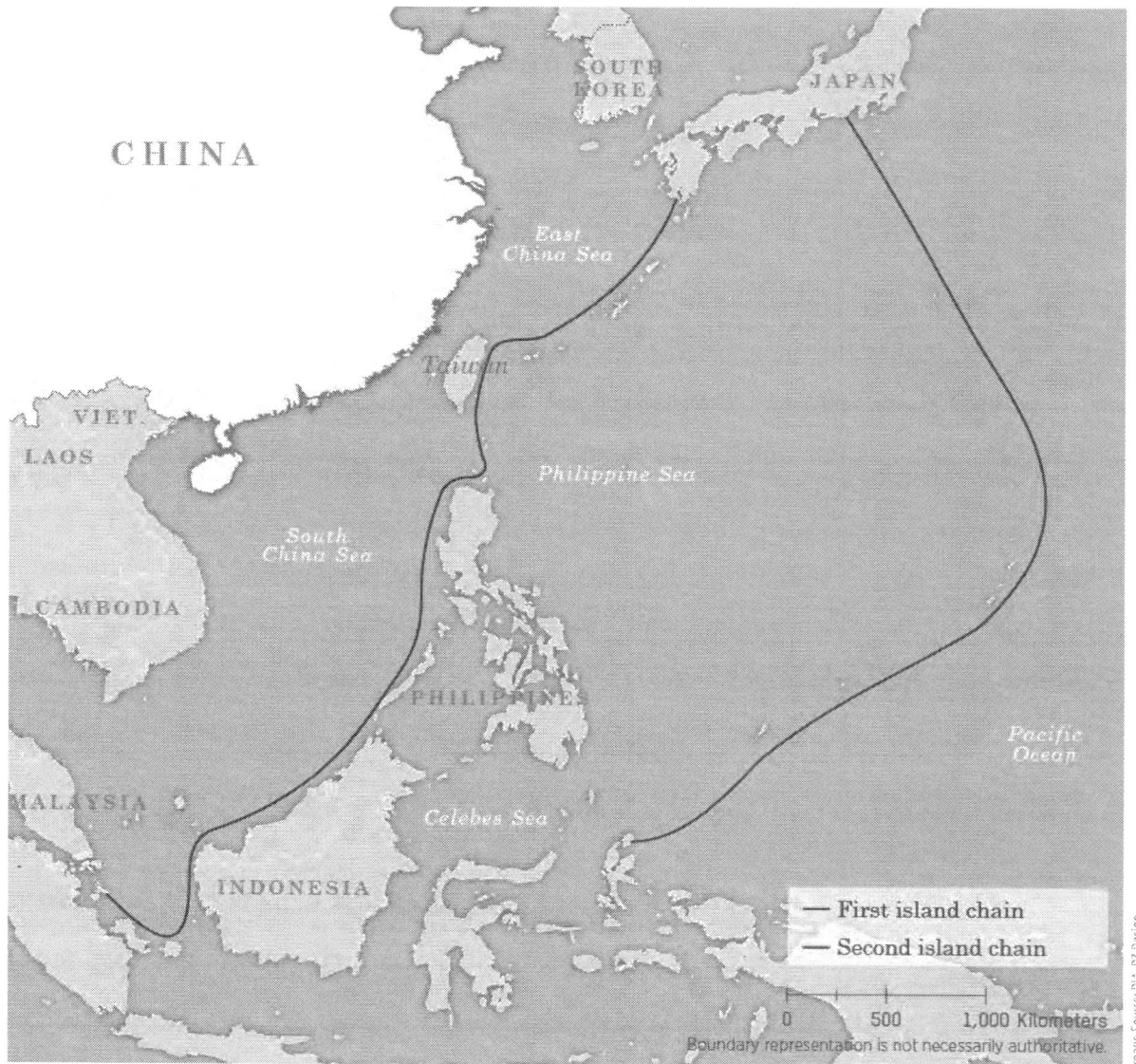

Image Source: DIA, D3 Design

Power Projection and Expeditionary Operations

Beijing's longstanding interest to eventually compel Taiwan's reunification with the mainland and deter any attempt by Taiwan to declare independence has served as the primary driver for China's military modernization. Beijing's anticipation that foreign forces would intervene in a Taiwan scenario led the PLA to develop a range of systems to deter and deny foreign regional force projection. The implementation of Hu's New Historic Missions in 2004 led to the incremental expansion of the military's modernization priorities to develop a PLA capable of operating in new domains and at increasing distances from the mainland. During this modernization process, PLA ground, air, naval, and missile forces have become increasingly able to project power during peacetime and in the event of regional conflicts. Beijing almost certainly will use this growing ability to project power to bolster international perceptions of its role as a regional power and global stakeholder.

Although Beijing states that its intent is to serve as a stabilizing force regionally, in practice the PLA's actions frequently result in increased tensions. Since 2012, Beijing has routinely challenged Tokyo's Senkaku Island claims in the East China Sea. China's Coast Guard frequently conducts incursions into the contiguous zone surrounding the islands to further China's claims, while its Navy operates around the claims to enforce administration. The PLA has expanded and militarized China's outposts in the South China Sea, and China's Coast Guard, backed by the PLAN, commonly harasses Philippine and Vietnamese ships in the region.

Examples of incremental improvements to PLA power projection in the region are readily found in annual military exercises and operations.[60] For instance, in 2015 the PLA Air Force (PLAAF) carried out four exercise training missions past the first island chain through the Bashi Channel, the northernmost passage of the Luzon Strait, and through the Miyako Strait closer to Japan. The Miyako Strait flights were 1,500 kilometers from Guam, within range of the PLAAF's CJ-20 air-launched land-attack cruise missile (LACM).[61] Also in 2015, the PLAAF began flying the H-6K medium-range bomber, the PLAAF's first aircraft capable of conducting strikes on Guam (with air-launched LACMs like the CJ-20), past the first island chain into the western Pacific.

China is also developing new capabilities that will enhance Beijing's ability to project power. In September 2016, then-PLAAF Commander Gen Ma Xiaotian confirmed for the first time that the PLAAF was developing a new long-range bomber that would undoubtedly exceed the range and capabilities of the H-6K. Although the H-6K recently began flying with LACMs, this Chinese-built airframe is the 10th design variant of the Soviet Tu-16, which began flying in 1952.[62] In 2016, China and Ukraine agreed to restart production of the world's largest transport aircraft, the An-225, which is capable of carrying a world-record payload of nearly 254 tons. China expects the first An-225 to be delivered and operational by 2019.[63] If used by the military, this capability would facilitate the PLA's global reach.

In addition to land-based aircraft, China is currently building its first domestically designed and produced aircraft carrier.[64] The primary purpose of this first domestic aircraft carrier will be to serve a regional defense mission. Beijing probably also will use the carrier to project power throughout the South China Sea and possibly into the Indian Ocean.[65] The carrier conducted initial sea trials in May 2018 and is expected to enter into service by 2019.[66] *[For more information on China's aircraft carrier program, please see Appendix B.]*

Other areas that reflect China's growing military presence abroad include China's participation in UN peacekeeping operations.[67] Separately, China routinely employs its modern hospital ship, *Peace Ark*, to support HADR missions worldwide. In 2015, the PLA conducted its first permissive noncombatant evacuation operation, to extricate Chinese and other civilians from Yemen supported by Yemeni security forces.

China's efforts to enhance its presence abroad, such as establishing its first foreign military base in Djibouti and boosting economic connectivity by reinvigorating the New Silk Road Economic Belt and 21st Century Maritime Road under the "Belt and Road Initiative" (BRI), could enable the PLA to project power at even greater distances from the Chinese mainland.[68,69,70] In 2017, China's leaders said that the BRI, which at first included economic initiatives in Asia, South Asia, Africa, and Europe, now encompasses all regions of the world, including the Arctic and Latin America, demonstrating the scope of Beijing's ambition.

Growing PLA mission areas and enhanced presence abroad may lead to an increase in demand for the PLA to protect China's overseas interests and provide support to Chinese personnel. China's increased presence also introduces the possibility that the PLA could play a more prominent role in delivering global public goods in the future.

PLAN Anwei class hospital ship *Heping Fangzhou (Peace Ark)*.

China's Southern Theater Forces

PLA Army
- Theater Army HQ
- Group Army HQ
- Infantry Division/Brigade*
- Armor Division/Brigade*
- Artillery Brigade
- Air Defense Brigade
- Amphibious Brigade
- Aviation Brigade
- Special Forces Brigade

PLA Air Force
- Theater Air Force HQ
- Base
- Fighter/Ground-Attack Brigade/Regiment**
- Bomber Division

PLA Rocket Force
- Missile Base
- Missile Unit

PLA Navy
- Theater Navy HQ
- Naval Aviation Division *(includes 3 subordinate regiments)*
- Marine Brigade
- Composite Flotilla
- Destroyer Flotilla
- Frigate Flotilla
- Landing Ship Flotilla
- Submarine Flotilla
- Theater boundary

*We anticipate a significant number of these maneuver units to become combined-arms brigades as part of PLA reforms.
**We anticipate fighter/ground-attack regiments will convert to brigades as part of PLA reforms.

China's Southern Theater forces are arrayed to support multiple contingencies.

Separately, China's modern naval platforms include advanced missile and technological capabilities that will strengthen the force's core warfighting competencies and enable credible combat operations beyond the reaches of land-based defenses. The expansion of naval operations beyond China's immediate vicinity will provide China with a diverse set of capabilities for striking targets across the Pacific and Indian Ocean regions, in addition to improving defensive capabilities such as exercising control of SLOCs. Improving bluewater capabilities will extend China's maritime security buffer to protect China's near- and far-seas interests more effectively.

China's current aircraft carrier and planned follow-on carriers will extend air defense umbrellas beyond the range of coastal systems and help enable task group operations in far seas. Sea-based land attack probably is an emerging requirement for the PLAN. Chinese military experts argue that to pursue a defensive strategy in far seas, the PLAN must improve its ability to control land from the sea through development of a long-range LACM.[71]

The PLA's land-based missile and air forces enable other military assets to focus on conducting offensive missions, such as blockades and sovereignty enforcement, as well as defensive operations farther from China's shores. China also focuses on enhancing the PLA's ISR capabilities, which will enable improved targeting and timely responses to perceived threats.

Nuclear Forces and Weapons

China invests considerable resources to maintain a limited, survivable nuclear force that can guarantee a damaging retaliatory strike.[72] [73] As part of this, China has long maintained a "no first use" (NFU) policy, stating it would use nuclear forces only in response to a nuclear strike against China.[74,75,76] There is some ambiguity, however, over the conditions under which China's NFU policy would apply. Some PLA officers have written publicly of the need to spell out conditions under which China might need to use nuclear weapons first; for example, if an enemy's conventional attack threatened the survival of China's nuclear force or of the regime itself.[77] Nevertheless, there has been no indication that national leaders are willing to attach such nuances and caveats to China's NFU doctrine.

The nuclear force is a strategic cornerstone for safeguarding national sovereignty and security. China has always pursued the policy of no first use of nuclear weapons and adhered to a self-defensive nuclear strategy. China unconditionally will not use or threaten to use nuclear weapons against non-nuclear-weapon states or in nuclear-weapons-free zones and will never enter into a nuclear arms race with any other country.

China will optimize its nuclear force structure; improve strategic early warning, command and control, missile penetration, rapid reaction, and survivability and protection; and deter other countries from using or threatening to use nuclear weapons against China.

—Excerpts from *China's Military Strategy*, May 2015

China is developing a new generation of mobile missiles, with warheads consisting of multiple independently targetable reentry vehicles (MIRVs) and penetration aids, intended to ensure the viability of its strategic deterrent in the face of continued advances in U.S. and, to a lesser extent, Russian strategic ISR, precision strike, and missile defense capabilities.[78] China is enhancing peacetime readiness levels for these nuclear forces to ensure responsiveness. China maintains nuclear-capable delivery systems in its Rocket Force and Navy. As of 2017, the Air Force had been reassigned a nuclear mission, probably with a developmental strategic bomber.[79,80,81,82,83] The bomber's deployment would provide China with its first credible nuclear triad of delivery systems dispersed across land, sea, and air—a posture considered since the Cold War to improve survivability and strategic deterrence.

PLA writings express the value of a "launch on warning" nuclear posture, an approach to deterrence that uses heightened readiness, improved surveillance, and streamlined decisionmaking processes to enable a more rapid response to enemy attack. These writings highlight the posture's consistency with China's NFU policy. China is working to develop a space-based early warning capability that could support this posture in the future.[84]

The PLA is developing a range of technologies to counter U.S. and other countries' ballistic missile defense systems, including maneuverable reentry vehicles (MARVs), MIRVs, decoys, chaff, jamming, thermal shielding, and hypersonic glide vehicles.[85,86,87] In addition, the PLA is likely to continue deploying more sophisticated C2 systems and refining C2 processes as growing numbers of mobile intercontinental ballistic missiles (ICBMs) and future nuclear-powered ballistic missile submarine (SSBN) deterrence patrols require the PLA to safeguard the integrity of nuclear release authority for a larger, more dispersed force.

China maintains a stockpile of nuclear warheads and continues research on and development and production of new nuclear weapons.[88] The PLA probably has multiple nuclear warhead designs that are decades old and require routine observation, maintenance, or refurbishment to maintain effectiveness.[89] China's nuclear weapon design and production organization—the China Academy of Engineering Physics—is the key organization in developing and maintaining China's nuclear force.[90] It employs tens of thousands of personnel, and its scientists are capable of conducting all aspects of nuclear weapon design research, including nuclear physics, materials science, electronics, explosives, and computer modeling.[91,92]

China Nuclear Weapon-Related Facilities

China's nuclear weapons program has been supported by a number of facilities that include production, processing, research and development, and testing.

China has the required industrial capacity to enrich uranium and produce plutonium for military needs. The China National Nuclear Corporation operates several uranium enrichment facilities organized under three plants.[93] China probably intends the bulk of its enrichment capacity to support its burgeoning nuclear power industry but could devote some enrichment capacity to support military needs.[94] China's plutonium production reactors probably ceased operation in the 1980s.[95] However, China's reprocessing facilities can extract plutonium from spent reactor fuel.[96]

Biological and Chemical Warfare

China has consistently claimed that it has never researched, produced, or possessed biological weapons and would never do so.[97] Beijing says China has researched only defensive biological technology necessary for China's defense.[98] China acceded to the Biological Weapons Convention (BWC) in 1984.[99] It declared the Academy of Military Science's Institute of Microbiology and Epidemiology in Beijing as a biodefense research facility.[100] China regularly and voluntarily submits to confidence-building measures under the BWC.[101] Although China is not a member of the Australia Group, China's export control regulations have been in line with Australia Group guidelines and control lists since 2002.[102, 103] China's biotechnology infrastructure is sufficient to produce some biological agents or toxins on a large scale.[104,105,106]

The Australia Group (AG) is an informal forum of countries which, through the harmonisation of export controls, seeks to ensure that exports do not contribute to the development of chemical or biological weapons. Coordination of national export control measures assists Australia Group participants to fulfil their obligations under the Chemical Weapons Convention and the Biological and Toxin Weapons Convention to the fullest extent possible.

—Excerpt from the Australia Group's website

China has declared that it once operated a small chemical weapons program for offensive purposes; however, Beijing has consistently maintained that the program was dismantled and all agents and munitions were used before China ratified the Chemical Weapons Convention (CWC) in 1997.[107] Beijing also has declared two historical chemical warfare production facilities that may have produced mustard gas, phosgene, and lewisite.[108,109] In 1998, Beijing published chemical export control regulations consistent with Organization for the Prohibition of Chemical Weapons (OPCW) standards. It also has consistently updated its chemical control list to reflect changes made to the Australia Group chemical control list. China continues to reaffirm its compliance with the CWC as well as its support for the activities conducted by the OPCW.[110,111,112] Since acceding to the CWC, China has declared hundreds of dual-use facilities and has hosted hundreds of facility inspections and OPCW-led seminars.[113,114]

China's chemical infrastructure is sufficient to research, develop, and produce some chemical agents on a large scale.[115]

China probably has the technical expertise to weaponize chemical and biological warfare (CBW) agents, and China's robust armaments industry and numerous conventional weapon systems, including missiles, rockets, and artillery, probably could be adapted to deliver CBW agents.[116] China has the technical expertise, military units, and equipment necessary to detect CBW agents and to defend against a CBW attack.[117]

Entities and individuals in China continue to supply countries of concern with technologies, components, and raw materials applicable to weapons of mass destruction and missile programs. Such material and technology transfers could assist countries in developing their own production capabilities.[118]

Space/Counterspace

Outer space has become a commanding height in international strategic competition. Countries concerned are developing their space forces and instruments, and the first signs of weaponization of outer space have appeared. China has all along advocated the peaceful use of outer space, opposed the weaponization of and arms race in outer space, and taken an active part in international space cooperation. China will keep abreast of the dynamics of outer space, deal with security threats and challenges in that domain, and secure its space assets to serve its national economic and social development, and maintain outer space security.

—Excerpt from *China's Military Strategy*, May 2015

The PLA historically has managed China's space program and continues to invest in improving China's capabilities in space-based ISR, satellite communication, satellite navigation, and meteorology, as well as human spaceflight and robotic space exploration.[119] China uses its on-orbit and ground-based assets to support national civil, economic, political, and military goals and objectives. Strategists in the PLA regard the ability to use space-based systems and deny them to adversaries as central to enabling modern informatized warfare. As a result, the PLA continues to strengthen its military space capabilities despite its public stance against the militarization of space. Space operations probably will form an integral component of other PLA campaigns and serve a key role in enabling actions to counter third-party intervention during military conflicts.

China continues to develop a variety of counterspace capabilities designed to limit or prevent an adversary's use of space-based assets during crisis or conflict. In addition to the research and possible development of satellite jammers and directed-energy weapons, China has probably made progress on kinetic energy weapons, including the anti-satellite missile system tested in July 2014.[120] China is employing more sophisticated satellite operations and probably is testing on-orbit dual-use technologies that could be applied to counterspace missions.

The PLA's Strategic Support Force (SSF), established in December 2015, has an important role in the management of China's aerospace warfare capabilities.[121] Consolidating the PLA's space, cyber, and electronic warfare capabilities into the SSF enables cross-domain synergy in "strategic frontiers." The SSF may also be responsible for research, development, testing, and fielding of certain "new concept" weapons, such as directed energy and kinetic energy weapons. The SSF's space function is primarily focused on satellite launch and operation to support PLA reconnaissance, navigation, and communication requirements. *[For more on the SSF, please see Appendix E.]*

Space and counterspace capabilities—like missile forces, advanced air and seapower, and cyber capabilities—are critical for China to fight and win modern military engagements. To support various requirements, China has built a vast ground and maritime infrastructure enabling spacecraft and space launch vehicle (SLV) manufacture, launch, C2, and data downlink.

Satellites

China employs a robust space-based ISR capability designed to enhance its worldwide situational awareness. Used for civil and military remote sensing and mapping, terrestrial and maritime surveillance, and military intelligence collection, China's ISR satellites are capable of providing electro-optical (EO) and synthetic aperture radar imagery, as well as electronic intelligence and signals intelligence data.[122]

China pursues parallel programs for military and commercial communications satellites (COMSATs), and owns and operates about 30 COMSATs used for civil, commercial, and military satellite communications. The PLA operates a small number of dedicated military COMSATs.[123] China's civil COMSATs incorporate turnkey off-the-shelf commercially manufactured components, and China produces its military-dedicated satellites domestically.[124] China continues to launch new COMSATs to replace its aging satellites and increase its overall satellite communications bandwidth, capacity, availability, and reliability.

China uses its domestically produced Dongfanghong-4 (DFH-4) satellite bus—the structure that contains the components of the satellite—for its military COMSATs.[125] Even though early satellites suffered mission-ending or mission-degrading failures, the DFH-4 has become a reliable satellite bus. The PLA and government continue to vigorously support the program and have signed numerous contracts with domestic and international customers for future DFH-4 COMSATs. The DFH-4 bus has also allowed China to position itself as a competitor in the international COMSAT market, orchestrating many contracts with foreign countries to supply on-orbit satellites, ground-control systems, and training.

In 2008, China launched the first Tianlian data-relay satellite of its China Tracking and Data Relay Satellite constellation. As of December 2017, China had four Tianlian data-relay satellites on orbit, allowing China to relay commands and data to and from its satellites even when those satellites were not over Chinese territory.

In 2000, China launched its first Beidou satellites to test the development of a regional satellite navigation system. By 2012, China had established a regional satellite navigation constellation consisting of 10 Beidou satellites and had initiated testing of a global constellation similar to the U.S. Global Positioning System (GPS).[126] As Beidou satellites continue to be placed in orbit, by 2020 China will complete its global constellation of 27 Beidou satellites while maintaining a separate regional constellation providing redundant coverage over Asia.[127]

China owns and operates 10 domestically produced Fengyun and Yunhai meteorological satellites.[128] The China Meteorological Administration supports civilian and military customers with the delivery of meteorological data and detailed weather forecasts. The newer satellites house almost a dozen all-weather sensors concerning atmospheric conditions as well as maritime terrain data for military and civilian customers. China's

Space operations control station.

membership in the World Meteorological Organization grants it free access to global meteorological data from the international organization's 191 members.[129]

Counterspace

The PLA is acquiring a range of technologies to improve China's counterspace capabilities. China is developing antisatellite capabilities, including research and possible development of directed-energy weapons and satellite jammers, and probably has made progress on the antisatellite missile system that it tested in July 2014. China is employing more sophisticated satellite operations and probably is testing dual-use technologies that could be applied to counterspace missions.[130]

China has not publicly acknowledged the existence of any new programs since it confirmed it used an antisatellite missile to destroy a weather satellite in 2007. PLA writings emphasize the necessity of "destroying, damaging, and interfering with the enemy's reconnaissance...and communications satellites," suggesting that such systems, as well as navigation and early warning satellites, could be among the targets of attacks designed to "blind and deafen the enemy."[131,132]

Long March-3B SLV in midlaunch.

Image Source: AFP

DEFENSE INTELLIGENCE AGENCY

Human Spaceflight and Space-Exploration Probes

China became the third country to achieve independent human spaceflight in 2003, when it successfully orbited the crewed Shenzhou-5 spacecraft, followed by space laboratory Tiangong-1 and -2 launches in 2011 and 2016, respectively. China intends to assemble and operate a permanently inhabited, modular space station capable of hosting foreign payloads and astronauts by 2022.[133]

43

China is the third country to have soft-landed a rover on the Moon, deploying the rover *Yutu* as part of the Chang'e-3 mission in 2013. China's Lunar Exploration Program plans to launch the first mission to land a rover on the lunar far side in 2018 (Chang'e-4), followed by its first lunar sample-return mission in 2019 (Chang'e-5).[134,135,136]

Space Launch

China has a robust fleet of launch vehicles to support its requirements. The Chang Zheng, or Long March, and Kuaizhou SLVs can launch Chinese spacecraft to any orbit.

Space Launch Sites

China operates four space launch sites: Jiuquan, Taiyuan, Xichang, and Wenchang.

Space Launch Fleet [137,138,139]

System	Propellant	Generation	Outlook
LM-2, LM-3, LM-4 series	Liquid	Legacy	Phase out by 2025
LM-5 series	Liquid	Next	Heavy-lift for the proposed space station and other payloads
LM-6	Liquid	Next	Light-lift for low Earth and sun-synchronous orbit
LM-7	Liquid	Next	Medium-lift for human spacefight and resupply to the future space station
LM-11 and Kuaizhou series	Solid	Next	Lift for emergency response

Cyberspace

Authoritative PLA writings identify controlling the "information domain"—sometimes referred to as "information dominance"—as a prerequisite for achieving victory in a modern war and as essential for countering outside intervention in a conflict.[140] The PLA's broader concept of the information domain and of information operations encompasses the network, electromagnetic, psychological, and intelligence domains, with the "network domain" and corresponding "network warfare" roughly analogous to the current U.S. concept of the cyber domain and cyberwarfare.[141]

The PLA Strategic Support Force (SSF) may be the first step in the development of a cyber-force by combining cyber reconnaissance, cyberattack, and cyberdefense capabilities into one organization to reduce bureaucratic hurdles and centralize command and control of PLA cyber units. Official pronouncements offer limited details on the organization's makeup or mission. President Xi simply said during the SSF founding ceremony on 31 December 2015 that the SSF is a "new-type combat force to maintain national security and [is] an important growth point for the PLA's combat capabilities."[142] The SSF probably was formed to consolidate cyber elements of the former PLA General Staff Third (Technical Reconnaissance) and Fourth (Electronic Countermeasures and Radar) Departments and Informatization Department.[143,144] *[For more information on the SSF, please see Appendix E.]*

> Cyberspace has become a new pillar of economic and social development, and a new domain of national security. As international strategic competition in cyberspace has been turning increasingly fiercer, quite a few countries are developing their cyber military forces. Being one of the major victims of hacker attacks, China is confronted with grave security threats to its cyber infrastructure. As cyberspace weighs more in military security, China will expedite the development of a cyberforce, and enhance its capabilities of cyberspace situation awareness, cyber defense, support for the country's endeavors in cyberspace and participation in international cyber cooperation, so as to stem major cyber crises, ensure national network and information security, and maintain national security and social stability.
>
> —Excerpt from *China's Military Strategy*, May 2015

The PLA could use its cyberwarfare capabilities to support military operations in three key areas. First, cyber reconnaissance allows the PLA to collect technical and operational data for intelligence and potential operational planning for cyberattacks because the accesses and tactics, techniques, and procedures for cyber reconnaissance translate into those also necessary to conduct cyberattacks. Second, the PLA could employ its cyberattack capabilities to establish information dominance in the early stages of a conflict to constrain an adversary's actions or slow mobilization and deployment by targeting network-based C2, C4ISR, logistics, and commercial activities. Third, cyberwarfare capabilities can serve as a force multiplier when coupled with conventional capabilities during a conflict.

PLA military writings detail the effectiveness of information operations and cyberwarfare in modern conflicts, and advocate targeting an adversary's C2 and logistics networks to affect the adversary's ability to operate during the early stages of conflict. One authoritative source identifies an adversary's C2 system as "the heart of information collection, control, and application on the battlefield. It is also the nerve center of the entire battlefield."[145] China's cyberwarfare could also focus on targeting links and nodes in an adversary's mobility system and identifying operational vulnerabilities in the mobilization and deployment phase.

The PLA also plays a role in cyber theft. In May 2014, the U.S. Department of Justice indicted five PLA officers on charges of hacking into the networks of U.S. companies for commercial gain. Beijing maintains that the Chinese government and military do not engage in cyberespionage and that the United States fabricated the charges.[146,147]

Denial and Deception

The PLA uses military deception to reduce the effectiveness of adversaries' reconnaissance and to deceive adversaries about the PLA's warfighting intentions, actions, or major targets.[148] PLA tradition emphasizes deception and psychological manipulation to create asymmetric advantages and enable surprise. The PLA has a longstanding doctrine for deception, and claims that it regularly practices deception during training. PLA sources describe military deception as a form of combat support, on par with ISR, meteorological support, missile calculation, engineering, and logistic support.

Denial and deception activities include: [149]

- Concealing and camouflaging.

- Blending false or misleading military movements with actual deployments and war preparations.

- Employing counterreconnaissance: understanding and evading, jamming, or destroying the whole spectrum of enemy reconnaissance activities against PLA units and facilities.

- Using deceptive maneuvers, psychological ploys, and unorthodox schemes to deceive, confuse, or otherwise manipulate an adversary into a militarily disadvantageous position. [150]

Skillfully employed, deception can paralyze an enemy force and achieve decisive results. Options range from no-warning strikes, violent multiaxis strikes, and envelopment to a less ambitious attempt to confuse the adversary regarding the exact timing, nature, direction, or scope of a PLA operation. [151,152]

Logistics and Defense-Industrial Modernization

[China's armed forces will] develop new support means, augment war reserves, integrate logistics information systems, improve rules and standards, and meticulously organize supply and support, so as to build a logistics system that can provide support for fighting and winning modern war, serve the modernization of the armed forces, and transform towards informatization.

—Excerpt from *China's Military Strategy*, May 2015

The PLA's increased focus on developing the capabilities required to conduct joint operations under "informatized" conditions that began in the 1990s has spurred efforts during the past two decades to develop the PLA's capacity to supply and sustain its operations. Along these lines, the PLA has taken steps to modernize its defense-industrial base to ensure that the PLA is developing capabilities to meet future mission requirements. Key areas of focus have included civil-military integration, support to joint combat operations, and high-tech weapons development.

Logistics

According to various military officials, the PLA's logistics system historically has been plagued with inefficiencies that degrade combat readiness and restrict its ability to support and sustain modern joint combat operations.[153,154,155] Since the late 1990s, the PLA has invested in the modernization of its logistics system, force structure, and supporting infrastructure to enable a transition from a rigid command-directed and manpower-dependent system, rife with corruption. The overarching objective of these reforms is to build a precision logistic support system that is capable of comprehensive, timely, and accurate logistic support to PLA joint operations.[156,157]

This transformation is dependent on building high-efficiency transportation and warehouse infrastructure, fielding new combat support equipment, integrating comprehensive information systems, and developing a new breed of officer capable of leveraging these capabilities to support rapid mobilization and high-tempo combat operations.[158,159] For China, logistics modernization also is heavily dependent on the PLA's ability to leverage the full potential of China's comprehensive national power to maximize combat capabilities, ensure peacetime efficiencies, and guarantee a constant state of combat readiness.[160]

The PLA has made great progress in logistics reform by improving logistics resources and procedures during the past two decades, and enhancing the PLA's ability to mobilize rapidly and project support along internal lines of communication for large operations (mostly disaster responses and exercises).[161,162,163,164] Since 2016, the PLA has implemented structural reforms to improve command and control, procedural reforms to improve civil-military integration, and oversight mechanisms to eliminate waste and inefficiencies that stem from longstanding corrupt practices within the logistics sector. The successful implementation of these measures remains to be seen, given the substantial cultural challenges of executing joint operations and reducing corruption.[165] The extent to which the PLA will be able to sustain external military force projection operations effectively also remains in question because the PLA's experience is still nascent. Efforts to support the PLA's first overseas military base, in Djibouti, may provide insight into these capabilities. *[Please see Appendix G for more information on PLA logistics.]*

Defense-Industrial Base

China's defense-industrial complex comprises both a military and a state sector governed by the CMC and State Council, respectively, under oversight of the Chinese Communist Party Central Committee.[166] The CMC's Equipment Development Department oversees weapons planning, research, development, and acquisition (RDA) in conjunction with the military service armament organizations for China's Army, Navy, Air Force, Rocket Force, Strategic Support Force, Armed Police, and Coast Guard.

The State Council's State Administration for Science, Technology, and Industry for National Defense (SASTIND) is the key organ responsible for overseeing China's state-owned defense-industrial corporations and enterprises.[167,168] Twelve SASTIND-subordinate defense-industrial enterprises conduct RDA and production in six distinct scientific, engineering, and technological domains:

- Aerospace/missile
- Naval/maritime
- Aviation
- Ground systems/ordnance
- Electronics
- Nuclear

During a speech at an equipment-quality work conference in 2015, CMC Vice Chairman General Xu Qiliang stressed the need to build a strong defense-industrial base to support military development. Xu emphasized themes of quality, innovation, technology, and improving combat readiness, but also said it would be necessary to strengthen laws, regulations, and accountability within the defense industry to increase quality standards.[169]

The PLA initiated defense-industrial reforms in 2016 that aimed to reduce bureaucracy, develop a more structured RDA and production decisionmaking apparatus, streamline developmental timelines, promote innovation, and institutionalize civil-military integration. Within an industrial context, the latter entails establishing a formal relationship between China's defense and civilian industrial bases to develop a technologically advanced, domestically reliant, and internationally relevant defense-industrial complex.[170] Key components of the initiative include the establishment of widely distributed "science cities," industrial parks, and high-tech zones—most near China's defense-industrial corporations and commercial industrial centers, large cities, and provincial capitals harboring significant RDA and manufacturing capabilities to facilitate efficient logistics and supply.[171,172] These reforms are expected to be implemented by 2020.

A key emphasis of defense-industrial reforms is developing an innovative military industrial complex capable of delivering cutting-edge technologies to meet future PLA requirements. China's research and development apparatus is designed to both identify and maximize the utility of emerging and potentially disruptive science and technology for military use. Scientific and technological disciplines with military applications targeted for development include hypersonics; nanotechnology; high-performance computing; quantum communications; space systems; autonomous systems; artificial intelligence; robotics; high-performance turbofan engine design; new, more efficient and powerful forms of propulsion; advanced manufacturing processes (including additive manufacturing/3-D printing); and advanced aerospace quality materials, just to name a few.[173]

Underground Facilities

The use of underground facilities for warfighting protection and concealment enhances China's military capacity, with particular emphasis on protecting C4I functions and missile assets. The PLA maintains a robust, technologically advanced underground facility (UGF) program. Given its NFU nuclear policy, China assumes it might have to absorb an initial nuclear strike while ensuring that leadership and strategic assets survive.

China determined in the mid-to-late 1980s that it needed to update and expand its military UGF program. This modernization effort took on a renewed urgency after China observed U.S. and coalition air operations during the 1991 Persian Gulf War and in the Balkans in 1999. The resultant emphasis on "winning high-tech battles" precipitated research into advanced tunneling and construction methods. These military campaigns convinced China it needed to build more survivable, deeply buried facilities, resulting in the widespread UGF construction effort we have detected throughout China for the past decade.

Missions Other Than War

The PLA views "nonwar" missions as a component of its readiness preparations, broader military modernization efforts, and military diplomacy. These operations also reflect the PLA's increasing role beyond China's borders.[174] In practice, the military shares many of these missions with the People's Armed Police, China's largely domestically oriented paramilitary force.

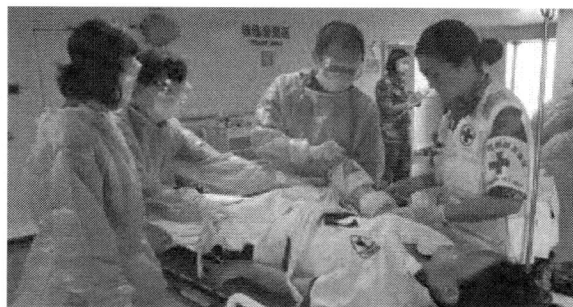

Medical team onboard *Peace Ark*.

China has broadened its participation in UN PKOs since 2008 to support foreign policy and military objectives by improving China's international image, providing the PLA with operational experience, and opening avenues for intelligence collection. China provides civilian police, military observers, engineers, logistic support specialists, and medical personnel to missions. In 2016, China had more than 3,000 peacekeepers deployed in support of 10 UN missions around the globe—the largest contingent of any permanent member nation of the UN Security Council—and separately committed to establish an additional 8,000-member peacekeeping standby force. China has trained about 500 foreign peacekeepers and has pledged to increase this number to 2,500 in the near future. In August 2017, Beijing announced that China's first helicopter unit to be deployed to a UN mission area had arrived in Sudan to support the United Nations African Union Mission in Darfur.[175] As of 2018, China has more than 2,500 troops, police, and military observers committed to UN missions.

Fulfilling international responsibilities and obligations. China's armed forces will continue to participate in UN peacekeeping missions, strictly observe the mandates of the UN Security Council, maintain its commitment to the peaceful settlement of conflicts, promote development and reconstruction, and safeguard regional peace and security. China's armed forces will continue to take an active part in international disaster rescue and humanitarian assistance, dispatch professional rescue teams to disaster-stricken areas for relief and disaster reduction, provide relief materials and medical aid, and strengthen international exchanges in the fields of rescue and disaster reduction. Through the aforementioned operations, the armed forces can also enhance their own capabilities and expertise.

—Excerpt from *China's Military Strategy*, May 2015

PLA soldiers working on a school in Thailand.

Image Source: DIMOC

Beijing's increased participation in UN PKO missions, particularly in terms of securing China's international image, has not come without costs. For instance, in 2016, after three Chinese peacekeepers were killed in action and six were wounded in two high-profile attacks in Mali and South Sudan, some international media reports accused Chinese peacekeepers of failing to interdict attacks on civilian foreign aid workers. These reports implicitly questioned China's ability to perform as a responsible global actor.

In 2017, China sustained its contributions to counterpiracy operations in the Gulf of Aden through the deployment of its 28th naval escort task force to the region since 2008. During the same period, the PLAN continued to use support for counterpiracy to justify Chinese submarine patrols to the Indian Ocean. In 2016, a nuclear-powered attack submarine conducted a port call in Karachi, Pakistan, during an official visit by the PLAN commander, marking China's first port call in South Asia by a nuclear submarine. In 2017, Chinese attack submarines conducted port calls in Seppangar, Malaysia, and Karachi, but Sri Lanka denied a port call request in Colombo.[176] These submarine patrols demonstrate the PLAN's emerging capability to protect China's SLOCs and to increase China's power projection into the Indian Ocean.

China continues to use humanitarian and disaster relief and counterterrorism cooperation as low-threat avenues to advance military engagement with many of its foreign partners. In March 2016, Beijing also proposed the creation of a maritime joint search and rescue hotline with the Association of Southeast Asian Nations, probably in part as a means of assuaging regional concerns over Chinese activities in the South China Sea.

Outlook: Developing a Robust Force

China's military modernization efforts have followed the broader growth and development of China as a whole. The PLA has made efforts toward reducing corruption, professionalizing training and education, developing a science and technology base for research and development, and organizing the force for effective C2. With its economic and security interests reaching around the globe, Beijing perceives further modernization of the PLA as an imperative for continued stability and security of its growing interests.

During the past decade alone, from counterpiracy operations in the Gulf of Aden to an expanded military presence in the East and South China Seas, China has demonstrated a willingness to use the PLA as an instrument of national power in the execution of "historic missions" in the new century. Improvements in PLA equipment and capabilities that have focused on generating combat power across the PLA services present Beijing with additional response options as China faces increasing global security concerns. Expected advances in areas such as nuclear deterrence, power projection, cyberspace, space, and electromagnetic spectrum operations will continue to be critical components of the PLA's developing capabilities. China also continues to develop capabilities for "nonwar" missions, such as HADR and counterpiracy.

In the coming years, the PLA is likely to grow even more technologically advanced, with equipment comparable to that of other modern militaries. The PLA will acquire advanced fighter aircraft, naval vessels, missile systems, and space and cyberspace assets as it organizes and trains to address 21st century threats farther from China's shores.

The world today is undergoing unprecedented changes, and China is at a critical stage of reform and development. In their endeavor to realize the Chinese Dream of great national rejuvenation, the Chinese people aspire to join hands with the rest of the world to maintain peace, pursue development, and share prosperity.

China's destiny is vitally interrelated with that of the world as a whole. A prosperous and stable world would provide China with opportunities, while China's peaceful development also offers an opportunity for the whole world. China will unswervingly follow the path of peaceful development, pursue an independent foreign policy of peace and a national defense policy that is defensive in nature, oppose hegemonism and power politics in all forms, and will never seek hegemony or expansion. China's armed forces will remain a staunch force in maintaining world peace.

Building a strong national defense and powerful armed forces is a strategic task of China's modernization drive and a security guarantee for China's peaceful development. Subordinate to and serving the national strategic goal, China's military strategy is an overarching guidance for blueprinting and directing the building and employment of the country's armed forces. At this new historical starting point, China's armed forces will adapt themselves to new changes in the national security environment, firmly follow the goal of the Communist Party of China to build a strong military for the new situation, implement the military strategic guideline of active defense in the new situation, accelerate the modernization of national defense and armed forces, resolutely safeguard China's sovereignty, security and development interests, and provide a strong guarantee for achieving the national strategic goal of the 'two centenaries' and for realizing the Chinese Dream of achieving the great rejuvenation of the Chinese nation.

—Excerpt from *China's Military Strategy*, May 2015

Note: The "two centenaries" is a reference to the 2021 centenary of the CCP as well as the 2049 centenary of the People's Republic of China.

APPENDIX A: PLA Army

The PLA Army (PLAA) is the world's largest standing ground force, with approximately 915,000 active-duty personnel in combat units.[177] China's military reforms since 2015 have included creating a separate PLAA headquarters for the first time in the PLA's history. In April 2017, the PLA announced the reduction of 5 of the PLAA's 18 group armies (corps-sized units), and the restructuring to a corps-brigade-battalion force structure. This new design implemented more mobile, modular units and integrated maneuver elements into combined-arms brigades.[178] The PLAA is also modernizing C4I systems to enhance its forces' interoperability.

Roles and Missions

The PLAA's role is to serve as the primary ground fighting force for the PLA. Accordingly, the PLAA's mission falls into five areas with eight supporting capabilities.

Roles and Missions

PLAA Strategic Purpose	
1	Respond to emergencies and military threats
2	Safeguard the sovereignty and security of China's territory, China's security interests in new domains, and overseas interests
3	Participate in security cooperation and maintain regional and world peace
4	Maintain China's political security and social stability
5	Perform emergency rescue and disaster relief

Required Tactical and Operational Capabilities			
1	Remote maneuver actions	5	Occupation and control actions
2	Information countermeasures	6	Regional guard actions
3	Firepower strike options	7	Special operations actions
4	Mobile assault actions	8	All-dimension defensive actions

Major Ground Units

Inset map: CHINA, MONGOLIA

78

RUSSIA

Northern Theater

79

NORTH KOREA

81 Beijing

82

Military Demarcation Line

80

SOUTH KOREA

Subordinate to Western Theater

Central Theater

Northern Theater

76

83

71

CHINA

72

Western Theater

77

Eastern Theater

Southern Theater

73

Taiwan

75

74

Hong Kong S.A.R.

Macau S.A.R.

VIETNAM

LAOS

0   250   500 Kilometers

Representations of locations are approximate.
Boundary representation is not necessarily authoritative.
Information current as of 01 Jan 2018.

South China Sea

Legend:
- Theater Army HQ
- (##) Group Army
- Airborne Corps
- Marine Corps HQ unlocated
- — Theater boundary

PLAA-produced publications consistently discuss "new-type operations," which are operations that emphasize an effects-based application of combat power to neutralize key nodes, diminish the enemy's capability to effectively fight (systems confrontation), and achieve operational objectives quickly. At the tactical level, PLAA battalion training most likely includes use of precise, long-range fire to maximize protection and surprise; dispersion of formations of weapon platforms while relying on advanced communications technologies; and increasingly lethal munitions to enable PLAA commanders to produce mass effects on an enemy.

Units

The development of the PLAA's "new-type" operational forces reflects China's desire to plan and construct a force that is multifaceted, with capabilities for operations ranging from high-intensity conflict to security-stability operations. These forces stress the importance of ISR and leveraging information to enable future combat; they can conduct three-dimensional operations (Army aviation, air mobility, and airborne forces) and can operate in a severely degraded communications environment.

Operations emphasize engaging the enemy from much longer distances, place greater importance on protection and survivability, and emphasize the employment of cyberoperations. Future PLAA units will be smaller, more modular, and less dependent on headquarters for resources.

The PLAA is the world's largest army.

Image Source: AFP

This new construct envisions generating combat power and effectiveness across warfighting functions, from smaller, more flexible units.[179]

In line with the strategic requirement of mobile operations and multidimensional offense and defense, the PLAA will continue to reorient from theater defense to transtheater mobility. In the process of building small, multifunctional and modular units, the PLAA will adapt itself to tasks in different regions, develop the capacity of its combat forces for different purposes, and construct a combat force structure for joint operations. The PLAA will elevate its capabilities for precise, multidimensional, transtheater, multifunctional, and sustainable operations.

—Excerpt from *China's Military Strategy*, May 2015

PLAA Units[180,181]

The table below highlights PLAA units by type and size.

Type and Echelon	
Army Groups	13
Combined-Arms Brigades	78
Artillery Brigades	15
Army Aviation/Air Assault Brigades	13
Mechanized Infantry Division	1

Armor and Infantry. The majority of the PLAA's armored and infantry units are organized as combined-arms brigades, but the PLAA maintains a few maneuver units organized into divisions. The combined-arms brigades vary in size and composition, containing up to 5,000 troops. Infantry units include motorized infantry (those equipped with trucks for transportation) as well as mechanized infantry units, which can be equipped with either wheeled or tracked armored infantry fighting vehicles. Equipment in PLAA infantry units varies and may include a mix of obsolete platforms from the 1960s up to some of the region's most modernized and capable platforms. PLAA armored units similarly comprise a wide range of legacy tanks and modernized third-generation main battle tanks.[182]

Artillery. Artillery is the key component of the PLAA's strike capability.[183] Its primary function is supporting ground assault missions, and artillery accounts for more than one-third of the Army's operational unit strength.[184] The current family of modernized systems emphasizes long-range deployment, firepower operations, and mobile warfare—the key attributes that the PLAA requires in its newest artillery systems.[185]

Air Defense. PLAA air defense units comprise active-duty forces and reserve forces. Active-duty units provide air defense for the mobile forces. These units are equipped with a mix of tactical antiaircraft missiles, antiaircraft artillery, antiaircraft gun and missile systems, and man-portable antiaircraft missile systems. An extensive reserve antiaircraft artillery force, comprising divisions and separate brigades, provides primarily area antiaircraft artillery protection for China's urban areas and critical economic areas.[186,187]

Electronic Countermeasures. Electronic countermeasure (ECM) units are equipped with a range of modern ground-based electronic warfare systems capable of targeting large portions of the electromagnetic spectrum. PLAA ECM units use HF/VHF/UHF, radar, and unmanned aerial vehicle (UAV)-borne jamming systems to support maneuver forces.

Special Operations Forces. Consistent with the PLAA's recent emphasis on information- and intelligence-driven operations, the PLAA's Special Operations Forces (SOF) have undergone substantial expansion. According to PLAA doctrine, SOF missions include "carrying out special reconnaissance, special sabotage, [and] harassment attacks; seizing and controlling key targets; guiding precision attacks; conducting rescues behind enemy lines; and dealing with border armed conflicts and unexpected events."[188] PLAA SOF appears to focus primarily on special reconnaissance and direct-action missions.[189]

Army Aviation. PLA Army Aviation comprises 13 brigades. These units are subordinate to corps-level units in the five theater commands. The PLA considers PLA Army Aviation a "new-type" operational force and a priority for modernization. Since 2010, PLA Army Aviation has transformed from an auxiliary transport role to that of a main combat force and has increased its regiments to brigade echelon. Newly fielded and forthcoming helicopters combined with structural and operational changes under way in the PLAA indicate a pattern of development designed to mold a three-dimensional, new-type Army Aviation force with all-weather day-or-night capability.[190]

Logistics and Support. PLAA logistics and equipment support elements exist in active and reserve units. They provide field forces with all classes of supply and maintenance support as well as medical and technical support. These forces normally form support groups under logistics and equipment command posts.[191]

The PLAA also relies heavily on civil-military integration to supplement services provided by military logistics units. Official publications note the importance of integrating civilian and military production during mobilizations, and the PLAA regularly uses a combination of military and civilian materiel (rations and fuel), equipment (civilian transport vehicles, vessels,

and aircraft), and facilities (ports, docks, and hospitals) during large-scale training exercises.

Equipment [192,193]

Main Battle Tanks. The PLAA armored corps comprises a mix of older, obsolete tanks and a variety of more modern tanks. The PLAA is modernizing its armored units by fielding third-generation tanks with updated armor packages, larger-caliber cannons, improved fire-control systems, and advanced electronics and communications. The most capable of these tanks are the Type 96A and Type 99 main battle tank.[194]

A ZTZ99 (Type 99) main battle tank conducting training.

Image Source: AFP

Armored Infantry Fighting Vehicles *(AIFVs) and Armored Personnel Carriers (APCs).* The PLAA has a large variety of wheeled and tracked AIFVs and APCs. Highlighted below are two of the PLAA's most modern AIFVs.

- ***ZBD-04A.*** The ZBD-04A is one of China's newest tracked AIFVs. It is well armed with a 100-mm gun, a coaxial 30-mm cannon, and a 7.62-mm machinegun. It has a traditional layout, with the engine in the front right and the driver in the front left. The turret is in the middle, with the troop compartment in the rear. The ZBD-04A has a licensed copy of the Russian BMP 3 turret. It has a three-member crew and room for seven passengers. This IFV weighs about 21 tons and has improved armor.

- **ZBL-09.** The ZBL-09, often referred to as a "wheeled light tank," is the PLA's newest wheeled armored vehicle. It has an 8x8 configuration, a 105-mm gun, a 7.62-mm coaxial machinegun, a 12.7-mm machinegun on the right side of the turret, and six 76-mm grenade launchers on each side of the turret. The driver is in the front, the turret is in the middle, the power pack is in the rear, and passive armor is fitted to the hull and turret.

Artillery and Rockets. China continues to produce modern artillery systems aimed at advancing the mechanization of PLAA artillery while integrating information systems to increase lethality and precision. The primary systems are the PHL03 300-mm self-propelled (SP) multiple rocket launcher, the PLZ05 155-mm SP gun/howitzer, and two tracked and two wheeled 122-mm artillery systems. These new systems are likely to replace almost all towed artillery. The exception to this modernization trend is PLAA coastal defense artillery, which will continue using towed Type 59-1 130-mm guns and Type 66 152-mm howitzers.

Air Defense. China has been fielding medium-range HQ-16 surface-to-air missiles (SAMs) with select air defense units in the PLAA as

PHL03 Multiple Rocket Launchers on parade in Beijing

Image Source: AFP

part of a comprehensive upgrade of its air defense capabilities. China manufactures its own variant of Russia's SA-15 and is fielding the system with PLAA air defense units supporting tracked armored forces.

China also manufactures a domestically designed variant of the French Crotale tactical SAM system. This wheeled SAM is being fielded with PLAA air defense units supporting primarily wheeled fighting forces. China's tactical SAMs have been replacing outdated large-caliber antiaircraft artillery in air defense units defending operational and large tactical-level units.

China is fielding a modern domestically produced SP antiaircraft gun system with select PLAA air defense units protecting larger maneuver units. The PGZ-07 will provide highly mobile coverage for headquarters areas, troop concentrations, and key logistic support areas.

PGZ-07 self-propelled antiaircraft system on parade in Beijing.

Image Source: AFP

China's domestically designed and produced PGZ-04 integrated missile-gun antiaircraft system is an upgraded version of the PGZ-95, equipped with more effective short-range SAMs. The system is fielded with many PLAA armored and mechanized units for close-range air defense protection of combat maneuver elements.

Training

In 2015, PLA leaders directed changes to ground forces training.[195] These changes included a call for increased emphasis on problem solving, innovation, and realistic combat training, replacing previously scripted training methods. Leaders stressed the performance of key tasks—such as conducting joint training, training in nighttime combat, and training under adverse weather and geographical conditions—as essential to winning wars. The PLAA makes use of a number of training locations available for its ground

forces and maintains at least one sizable training area in each of China's military theaters. These training areas offer a variety of terrain, from coastal and flat areas to moderately hilly, to high plateau and mountainous terrains. The major training bases provide units with venues featuring large areas for field maneuvers, artillery fires, and force-on-force confrontations.

Professionalization. Since at least 2012, PLAA units ("red forces") rotating through combined-arms training centers have trained against a permanently established "blue force," also known as an opposition force.[196] The construction of a blue force was undertaken to ensure that the PLAA would become more sophisticated in conducting realistic training scenarios. Increasingly, PLAA training emphasizes the need to empower lower-level leaders to conduct target-based, opportunistic, initiative-driven combat. The PLAA has decreased the emphasis on "saving face," shifting toward a culture of understanding that commanders and subordinates should be allowed—and expected—to make mistakes in training.

Recruitment and Professional Military Education. Military service probably will remain a less attractive career option if China's economy stays healthy. Although Chinese youth remain interested in the career field, interest is not widespread.[197] The PLAA relies on a 2-year conscription period along with a mix of volunteers (the ratio of conscripts to volunteers is unclear). Recruitment challenges notwithstanding, the PLA continues to pursue efforts to "cultivate new-type military personnel" to retain talent and develop personnel who can meet the data demands of modern warfare.[198] The Army also has changed military recruitment schedules and age limits in an effort to better attract educated and talented people.[199] Basic training, where students learn fundamental military skills and receive political indoctrination, continues to serve as the foundation for both conscripted and volunteer personnel entering the service. After completing the initial curriculum, trainees are sent to their respective units for additional on-the-job training. Some new soldiers will go on to different locations for technical training outside their assigned units.[200]

PLA cadets receive political instruction.

APPENDIX B: PLA Navy

The PLA Navy (PLAN) is Asia's largest navy, with an inventory of more than 300 surface combatants, submarines, amphibious ships, patrol craft, and specialized units.[201] The PLAN is rapidly replacing obsolescent, generally single-purpose ships in favor of larger, multirole combatants with advanced antiship, antiair, and antisubmarine weapons and sensors. This modernization aligns with China's growing emphasis on the maritime domain, with increasing demands on the PLAN to conduct operational tasks at increasing distances from the Chinese mainland using multimission, long-range, sustainable naval platforms with robust self-defense capabilities.[202,203]

In the 1980s, China's threat perceptions and growing economic interests drove a major shift in the strategic orientation and utility of naval forces. In particular, Chinese naval strategists sought to expand the bounds of their maritime capabilities beyond coastal defense. By 1987, PLAN Commander Adm Liu Huaqing had established a strategy referred to as "offshore defense."[204]

Although Liu characterized offshore areas as east of Taiwan and the northern part of the Pacific Ocean, stretching beyond the first island chain, offshore defense was often associated with operations in the Yellow Sea, East China Sea, and South China Sea—China's "near seas." Development of offshore defense paralleled the CMC's adoption of a new military strategy that focused on local wars on China's periphery rather than a major confrontation with the Soviet Union, and it focused on achieving regional goals and deterring a modern adversary from intervening in a regional conflict.

> In line with the strategic requirement of offshore waters defense and open-seas protection, the PLAN will gradually shift its focus from "offshore waters defense" to the combination of "offshore waters defense" with "open-seas protection," and build a combined, multifunctional and efficient marine combat force structure. The PLAN will enhance its capabilities for strategic deterrence and counterattack, maritime maneuvers, joint operations at sea, comprehensive defense, and comprehensive support.
>
> —Excerpt from *China's Military Strategy*, May 2015

Former President Hu and President Xi have repeatedly emphasized the importance of maritime power. In 2004, former President Hu's outline of the PLA's New Historic Missions encompassed new expectations for the PLAN. In his report to the 18th Party Congress in 2012, Hu declared, "We should enhance our capacity for exploiting marine resources, resolutely safeguard China's maritime rights and interests, and build China into a maritime power." Hu's public emphasis on maritime power and the need to "resolutely safeguard" China's maritime rights and interests reflect a growing consensus in China that maritime power is essential to advancing China's interests. This trajectory was carried forward under Xi and is explicit in China's 2015 military strategy:

> The traditional mentality that land outweighs sea must be abandoned, and great importance has to be attached to managing the seas and oceans and protecting maritime rights and interests. It is necessary for China to develop a modern maritime military force structure commensurate with its national security and development interests, safeguard its national sovereignty and maritime rights and interests, protect the security of strategic SLOCs (sea lines of communication) and overseas interests, and participate in international maritime cooperation so as to provide strategic support for building itself into a maritime power.
>
> —Excerpt from *China's Military Strategy*, May 2015

In 2015, Beijing formally introduced a new naval strategy, known as Offshore Defense and Open Seas Protection. The new strategy contains the primary elements of offshore defense but extends China's maritime sphere of operations beyond the first and second island chains and into the high seas in support of China's growing international interests and maritime missions. China relies heavily on maritime trade, access to overseas energy resources, and overseas employment of Chinese citizens to propel its domestic economy, spurring Beijing's concern for ensuring that the PLAN is capable

PLAN Jiangkai II class guided-missile frigate *Linyi*.

of pursuing open-seas protection missions. The PLAN's acquisition patterns demonstrate a growing emphasis on ships that are multimission capable and large enough to sustain these types of operations.

Roles and Missions

Given China's heavy reliance on maritime commerce, Beijing now has a vested interest in ensuring the security of international trade. Beijing also faces growing pressure to contribute to international security missions. As an increasingly modern and flexible force, the PLAN is at the forefront of addressing a number of enduring Chinese security challenges, from reunification with Taiwan to asserting China's maritime claims in the East and South China Seas. Today the PLAN's primary operational, training, and planning focus remains in the near seas, where China faces sovereignty disputes over various islands, maritime features, territorial waters, and associated maritime rights. The growth of China's diversified "nonwar" missions, including HADR, SLOC protection, and PKOs, has been a major driver of—and justification for—China's expanded naval strategy and operations in the far seas. The following subsections highlight a few of these missions.

The aircraft carrier *Liaoning* sailing in a formation of PLAN ships.

Countering Third-Party Intervention. Since the mid-1990s, Chinese planners and strategists have understood that the PLAN's development of capabilities to deter, delay, and if necessary degrade third-party forces' intervention in a time of conflict is essential. Nearly two decades later, China has closed many of the gaps in key warfare areas, such as air defense and long-range strike, that would support countering third-party forces in regional campaigns. China has built or acquired a wide array of advanced platforms, including submarines,

major surface combatants, missile patrol craft, maritime strike aircraft, and land-based systems that employ new, sophisticated antiship cruise missiles and SAMs. China also has developed the world's first roadmobile, antiship ballistic missile, a system specifically designed to attack enemy aircraft carriers. China's leaders hope that possessing these military capabilities will deter proindependence moves by Taiwan or, should deterrence fail, will permit a range of tailored military options against Taiwan and potential third-party military intervention.

Protecting Maritime Sovereignty. A key role for the PLAN is protecting China's maritime sovereignty. In the East and South China Seas, Beijing faces longstanding disputes with its neighbors regarding maritime boundaries, economic rights, and sovereignty over various geographic features. During the past few years, maritime disputes between China and rival claimants, including Japan, the Philippines, Vietnam, and Malaysia, have periodically intensified.

China's Navy, Coast Guard, and Maritime Militia are increasingly visible throughout the region, and Beijing has employed increasingly coercive tactics to advance its regional interests. As China's naval capabilities have grown, Beijing has taken steps to consolidate its maritime forces and improve its ability to respond flexibly to contingencies, while avoiding escalation to military conflict and maintaining a veneer of advancing peaceful global interests. China's land reclamation and outpost expansion in the Paracel and Spratly Islands include port facilities from which it can surge PLAN,

China Coast Guard (CCG), and People's Armed Forces Maritime Militia (PAFMM) ships to better enforce maritime sovereignty claims, as well as airbases to support reconnaissance, fighter, and strike aircraft.

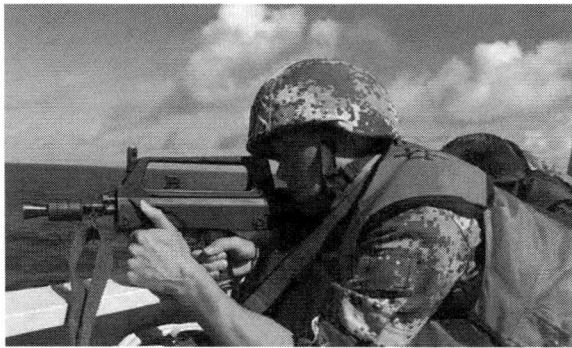

PLAN sailor participating in visit, board, search, and seizure (VBSS) training.

Under Chinese law, maritime sovereignty is a domestic law enforcement issue under the purview of the CCG. Beijing also prefers to use CCG ships for assertive actions in disputed waters to reduce the risk of escalation and to portray itself more benignly to an international audience. For situations that Beijing perceives carry a heightened risk of escalation, it often deploys PLAN combatants in close proximity for rapid intervention if necessary. China also relies on the PAFMM – a paramilitary force of fishing boats – for sovereignty enforcement actions.

Sea Lane Protection. China increasingly sees a need for the PLAN to help protect its economic investments and political interests around the world. The security of oil import routes from the Middle East and Africa that pass through the Indian Ocean is particularly vital to China. Large portions of China's critical mineral imports and trade in manufactured products and components also use these routes. Since any disruption of China's trade could undermine China's economy, the PLAN is placing growing importance on developing long-range SLOC protection and general naval presence capabilities. For example, SLOC protection and naval presence missions are among the main drivers in China's establishment of a naval logistics support base in Djibouti as well as Beijing's pursuit of additional logistics-port-access agreements. In addition, the PLAN's participation in counterpiracy operations in the Gulf of Aden demonstrates Beijing's intention to protect important SLOCs.

Naval Diplomacy. Another growing PLAN mission is naval diplomacy. Since PLAN task groups began supporting counterpiracy operations in the Gulf of Aden in 2008, the returning units have often followed the deployment with port visits across the Indian Ocean and other regions. In 2017, the PLAN completed its longest goodwill deployment in October, visiting 20 countries in 7 months, including several port calls in Europe. The PLAN also employs its hospital ship, *Peace Ark*, to support HADR missions worldwide. These visits advance the Navy's international profile, provide opportunities for bilateral cooperation, and build the PLAN's experience in areas farther from China's coast.

PLAN Luyang II class destroyer *Xian.*

Image Source: DIMOC

Nontraditional Missions. In 2004, the PLAN was tasked with safeguarding China's national development and playing an important role in ensuring world peace. This represented a substantial adjustment to China's national defense strategy and broadened its definition of security to include new geographic and functional areas beyond the PLA's traditional territorial security missions. Missions such as naval escort in the Gulf of Aden support China's economic interests while enhancing China's international image.

Units

The PLAN controls all of China's naval and naval aviation forces as well as seven marine brigades and has deployed naval forces in three of China's five geographically oriented theaters that conduct day-to-day operations. The deputy commander of each fleet commands its respective aviation force. The 2015 PLA-wide structural reforms formally separated operational control of the Navy from force-building aspects administered by PLAN headquarters, and additional changes to the PLAN's structure, particularly at the fleet level and below, are expected in 2018.

DEFENSE INTELLIGENCE AGENCY

67

Major Naval Units

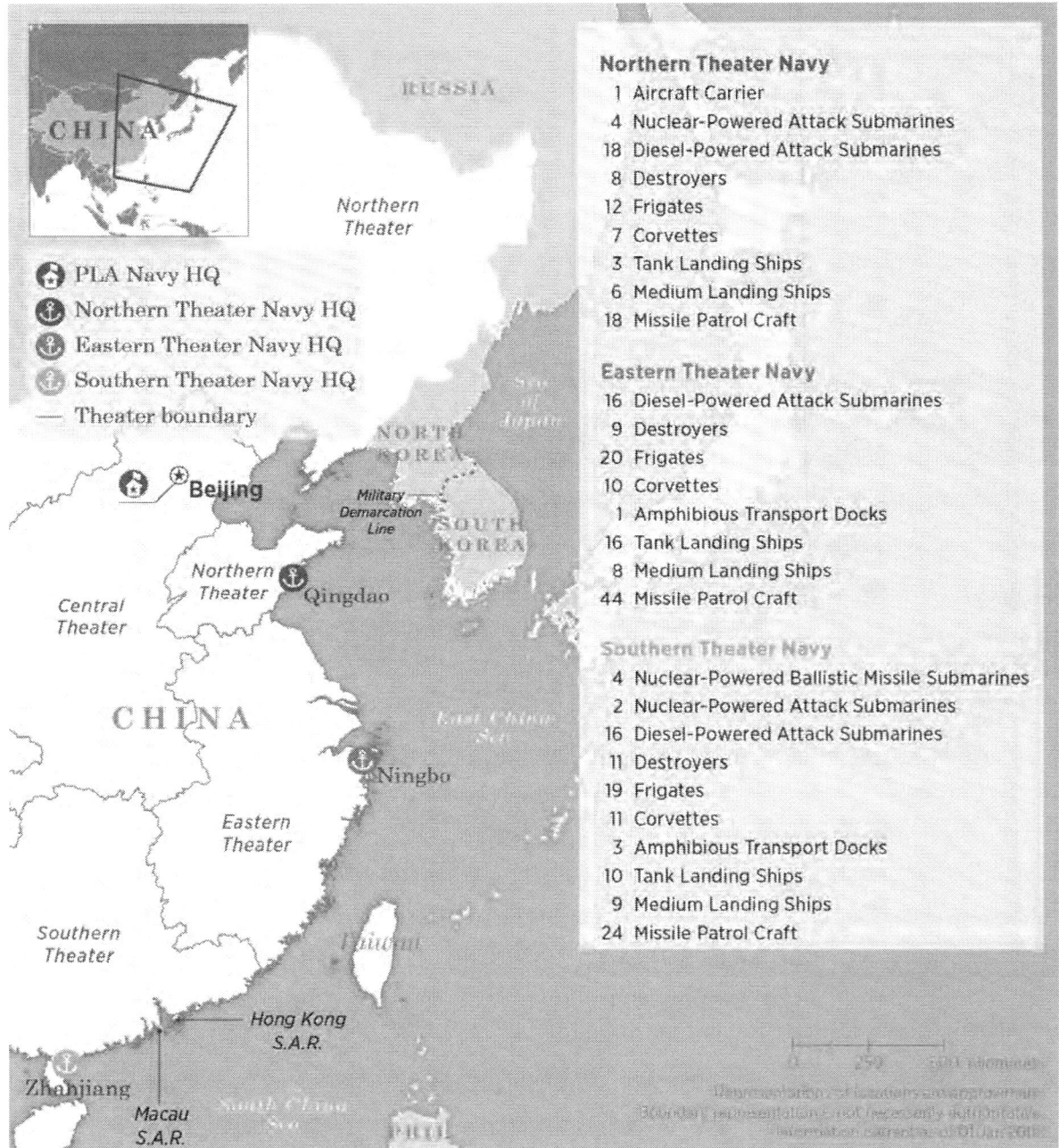

PLA Navy HQ
Northern Theater Navy HQ
Eastern Theater Navy HQ
Southern Theater Navy HQ
— Theater boundary

Northern Theater Navy

  1 Aircraft Carrier
  4 Nuclear-Powered Attack Submarines
 18 Diesel-Powered Attack Submarines
  8 Destroyers
 12 Frigates
  7 Corvettes
  3 Tank Landing Ships
  6 Medium Landing Ships
 18 Missile Patrol Craft

Eastern Theater Navy

 16 Diesel-Powered Attack Submarines
  9 Destroyers
 20 Frigates
 10 Corvettes
  1 Amphibious Transport Docks
 16 Tank Landing Ships
  8 Medium Landing Ships
 44 Missile Patrol Craft

Southern Theater Navy

  4 Nuclear-Powered Ballistic Missile Submarines
  2 Nuclear-Powered Attack Submarines
 16 Diesel-Powered Attack Submarines
 11 Destroyers
 19 Frigates
 11 Corvettes
  3 Amphibious Transport Docks
 10 Tank Landing Ships
  9 Medium Landing Ships
 24 Missile Patrol Craft

North Sea Fleet. Headquartered in Qingdao, the North Sea Fleet is responsible for the Bo Hai, Yellow Sea, and northern portion of the East China Sea. It falls under the PLA Northern Theater Command's area of operations.

East Sea Fleet. Headquartered in Ningbo, the East Sea Fleet covers the majority of the East China Sea and the Taiwan Strait. It falls under the PLA Eastern Theater Command's area of operations.

South Sea Fleet. Headquartered in Zhanjiang, the South Sea Fleet is responsible for the South China Sea. It falls under the PLA Southern Theater Command's area of operations.

Equipment: Building a Modern Navy

During the past 15 years, China's naval modernization has produced a technologically advanced, flexible force structure. The PLAN has more than 300 surface combatants, submarines, amphibious ships, and missile-armed patrol craft. Although the overall inventory

Artist rendition of a PLAN Renhai class cruiser.

has remained relatively constant, the PLAN is rapidly retiring older, single-mission warships in favor of larger, multimission ships equipped with advanced antiship, antiair, and antisubmarine weapons and sensors and C2 facilities.

In the initial stages of its modernization, the PLAN successfully concentrated resources on improving its antisurface warfare (ASUW) capabilities, both in surface ship and submarine development. Subsequent efforts have focused on improving antiair warfare capabilities and providing modest improvements in antisubmarine warfare (ASW) capabilities.

Every major PLAN surface combatant under construction is capable of embarking a helicopter to support over-the-horizon targeting, ASW, and search and rescue. Meanwhile, the PLAN's submarine force remains largely concentrated on ASUW, with Jin class SSBNs poised to contribute to China's nuclear deterrent once they begin strategic patrols in the near future. Naval aviation is expanding its mission set by incorporating modern multirole combat aircraft along with modern special mission aircraft, carrier aviation, and UAVs. As a whole, the PLAN is becoming a force able to execute a wide variety of missions near home and far away.

Surface Force. In the late 1990s to early 2000s, the PLAN transitioned from a "green-water" (coastal) force to one capable of operating offshore with increasing regularity. During this period, China imported several major combatants, weapon systems, and sensors from Russia while concurrently producing and developing its own designs and modernizing older ships to employ advanced weapons. By the second decade of the 2000s, the PLAN was using Chinese designs for surface ships primarily equipped with Chinese weapons and sensors (although some engineering components and subsystems remained imported or license-produced in country at the time). Furthermore, the era of past designs has given way to production of modern multimission destroyer, frigate, and corvette classes as China's technological advancement in naval design has begun to approach a level commensurate with, and in some cases exceeding, that of other modern navies. Once operational, the new Renhai class (Type 055) guided-missile cruiser, of which several are currently under construction, will be one of the most advanced and powerful ships in the world, boasting a large array of advanced-capability weapons and sensors developed domestically.[205]

Shipboard air defense and antisurface warfare capabilities are arguably the most notable areas of improvement on PLAN surface ships. China has retired several older destroyers and frigates that had at most a point air defense capability and a range of just several nautical miles. Newer ships entering the force are equipped with medium- to long-range area air defense missiles, including the Renhai, which has 112 vertical-launch cells for mixed munitions. The PLAN received a total of six Luyang II (Type 052C) class guided-missile destroyers with the HHQ-9 SAM (55-NM range) and YJ-62 antiship cruise missiles (ASCMs) (150-NM range), and six Luyang III (Type 052D) class guided-missile destroyers are now operational, with several more under construction. The Luyang III carries an extended-range variant of the HHQ-9 SAM and YJ-18 ASCM (290-NM range). In addition, more than 25 Jiangkai II (Type 054A) class guided-missile frigates are now operational, with the vertically launched HHQ-16 (20- to 40-NM range), and more are under construction.[206]

These newer ships use modern combat management systems and air surveillance sensors, such as the Sea Eagle and Dragon Eye phased-array radars. These new units allow the PLAN surface force to operate outside shore-based air defense systems because one or two ships are equipped to provide air defense for the entire task group.

China's amphibious ship force has slowly grown since a modernization program began in the early 2000s. Since 2005, China has built six large Yuzhao (Type 071) class amphibious transport docks, signaling China's development of an expeditionary warfare and over-the-horizon amphibious assault capability as well as inherent HADR and counterpiracy capabilities. The Yuzhao can carry up to four of the new Yuyi air-cushion utility landing craft (similar to the U.S. landing craft air cushion, LCAC) as well as four or more helicopters, armored vehicles, and troops on long-distance deployments. Additional Yuzhao construction is expected in the near term, as is a follow-on amphibious assault ship (landing helicopter assault, LHA, which Chinese sources term the

The PLA Navy: Naval SAM Ranges

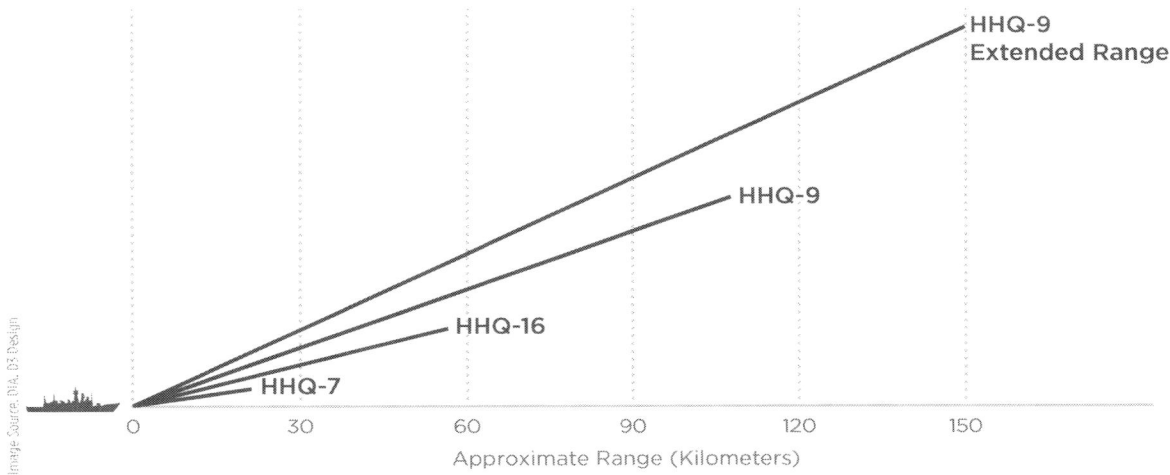

HHQ-9
Extended Range

HHQ-9

HHQ-16

HHQ-7

Approximate Range (Kilometers)

0   30   60   90   120   150

Image Source: DIA, DX Design

"Type 075") that not only is larger but incorporates a full flight deck for helicopters. Production on the LHA is expected to begin soon, if it has not already begun.

An expanded set of missions farther into the western Pacific Ocean and Indian Ocean, such as counterpiracy deployments, HADR missions, survey voyages, and goodwill port visits, has increased demands on and broadened the experience of the PLAN's fleet of ocean-going replenishment and service vessels. The PLAN recently launched two new Fuyi class fast combat support ships, intended to support aircraft carrier battle groups, as well as the smaller Fuchi class replenishment oilers, which support surface action groups and long-distance deployments. These ships constantly rotate in support of China's Gulf of Aden counterpiracy deployments and regularly accompany surface groups operating beyond the first island chain. At present, China has at least 10 fleet replenishment ships operational, with more under construction.

PLAN ships conducting replenishment at sea.

In addition, China has added a variety of oceangoing auxiliary ships in recent years, including submarine rescue ships, hospital ships, salvage and rescue ships, survey ships, intelligence collection ships, and various large transport ships.

PLAN sailors conduct VBSS training.

Submarine Force. China's modernizing force includes several types of submarines. For its diesel-electric force alone, between 2000 and 2005 China constructed Ming diesel attack submarines (SSs) and Song SSs and the first Yuan air-independent attack submarine (SSP), and purchased eight Kilo SSs from Russia. Although all of these classes remain in service, only the Yuan SSP is in production. Over time, reducing the number of classes in service helps streamline maintenance, training, and interoperability. The submarine force comprises 6 nuclear attack submarines, 4 nuclear-powered ballistic missile submarines, and 50 diesel attack submarines. By 2020 the submarine force probably will increase to about 70 submarines.

The Yuan SSP is China's most modern conventionally powered submarine. Seventeen are in service, with possibly three more slated for production. The Yuan SSP's combat capability is comparable to that of the Song; both can launch Chinese-built antiship cruise missiles, but the Yuan has the added benefit of an air-independent propulsion (AIP) system and may have incorporated quieting technology from the Russian-designed Kilo SS. The AIP system provides a submarine a source of power other than battery or diesel engines while still submerged, increasing its underwater endurance and reducing its vulnerability to detection.

The remainder of the conventional submarine force is a mix of Song, Ming, and Russian-built Kilo SSs. Of these, only the Ming and four of the older Kilos lack an ability to launch ASCMs. Eight of China's 12 Kilos are equipped with the SS-N-27 ASCM, which provides a long-range ASUW capability out to about 120 nautical miles. China's newest domestic submarine-launched ASCM, the CH-SS-N-13, extends a similar capability to the Song, Yuan, and Shang classes.

China also continues to modernize its nuclear-powered attack submarine force, although these make up a small percentage of the total number of submarines. Two Shang nuclear-powered attack submarines (SSNs) have been launched, one each in 2002 and 2003. After nearly 10 years, China is continuing production with four additional hulls of an improved Shang variant. These six submarines will replace the aging Han SSN on a nearly one-for-one basis during the next several years. After the completion of the improved Shang SSN, the PLAN is expected to begin production on another modified variant of the Shang SSN class, the Type 093B.[207] Thereafter, the PLAN probably will progress to the Type 095 nuclear-powered cruise missile submarine (SSGN). This class of submarine may provide a generational improvement in many areas, such as quieting and weapons capacity.

The PLA Navy's Jin class nuclear powered ballistic missile submarines, armed with the JL-2 submarine launched ballistic missile, provide China its first viable sea-based nuclear deterrent and credible second-strike nuclear capability. The JL-2 submarine-launched ballistic missile (SLBM) has nearly three times the range of the Xia SSBN's JL-1 SLBM, which was able to reach targets only in China's immediate vicinity. The JL-2 SLBM underwent successful testing in 2012. The Jin/JL-2 weapon system will provide China with a capability to strike targets in the continental United States from some patrol areas. To maintain a continuous at-sea nuclear deterrent, the PLAN probably would require a minimum of five Jin SSBNs; four are in service.

Aviation. The role of PLAN aviation has evolved during the past decade. PLAN combatants can now reach farther from shore and are more capable of providing their own air defense. This has allowed the PLAN to concentrate on an expanded array of aerial missions, particularly maritime strike, as well as maritime patrol, ASW, airborne early warn-

The JL-2/CSS-NX-14 SLBM in midlaunch.

Image Source: DIBMAC Report

ing (AEW), and logistics. China's first aircraft carrier signaled a new age for PLAN aviation, which is now evolving from an almost exclusively land-based force to one with a sea-based component.

Fixed-Wing Aircraft. During the past two decades, the PLAN has replaced antiquated fixed-wing aircraft, such as the Q-5 Fantan and the H-5 Beagle, with an array of high-quality aircraft. The force is now equipped for a wide range of missions, including offshore air defense, maritime strike, maritime patrol/ASW, and carrier-based operations. Just a decade ago, this air modernization relied very heavily on Russian imports. Following in the PLAAF's footsteps, the PLAN is now benefiting from domestic combat aircraft production. Today, the PLAN is taking deliveries of modern, domestically produced fourth-generation fighter aircraft, such as the J-10A Vigorous Dragon and the domestically produced J-11B Flanker. Equipped with modern radars and glass cockpits and armed with PL-8 and PL-12 air-to-air missiles, PLAN J-10As and J-11Bs are among the most modern aircraft in China's inventory and are capable of extended fighter patrols beyond China's coastal areas.

For maritime strike, the PLAN has relied on variants of the H-6 Badger bomber for decades. The H-6 is a licensed copy of the ex-Soviet Tu-16 Badger medium jet bomber, and maritime versions employ advanced ASCMs against surface targets. Despite the age of their design, the H-6s continue to receive electronics and payload upgrades, keeping the aircraft viable as a long-range strike platform. As many as 30 aircraft remain in service. Noted improvements for the upgraded Badger include the ability to carry a maximum of four ASCMs (instead of the two previously seen on earlier H-6D variants). The PLAN also has modified a few H-6s to serve as tankers, increasing the range of PLAN fighter aircraft.

With at least five regiments fielded across the three fleets, the JH-7 Flounder augments the H-6 as the workhorse of the PLAN's airborne maritime strike force. The JH-7 is a domestically produced tandem-seat fighter-bomber developed as a replacement for obsolete Q-5 Fantan light attack aircraft and H-5 Beagle bombers. Updated versions of the JH-7 feature a more capable radar and additional weapons capacity, enhancing its maritime strike capabilities. The JH-7 can carry up to four ASCMs and two PL-5 or PL-8 short-range air-to-air missiles, providing considerable payload for maritime strike missions, or the JH-7 can sacrifice two ASCMs for underwing fuel tanks, increasing the platform's range.

In addition to combat aircraft, the PLAN is expanding its inventory of fixed-wing maritime patrol aircraft, AEW, and surveillance aircraft. China has achieved significant new capabilities by modifying several existing airframes. The Y-8, a Chinese license-produced version of the ex-Soviet An-12 Cub, forms the basic airframe for several PLAN special-mission variants. All of these aircraft play a key role in providing a clear picture of surface and air contacts in the maritime environment. As the PLAN pushes farther from the coast, long-range aircraft capable of extended onstation times to act as the fleet's eyes and ears become increasingly important.

The PLAN has also developed a Y-9 ASW variant. The new aircraft is equipped with a magnetic anomaly detector boom, similar to that of the U.S. Navy's P-3. This Y-9 ASW variant is equipped with surface-search radar mounted under the nose as well as multiple-blade antennas on the fuselage, probably for electronic surveillance. A small EO/infrared turret is located just behind the nose wheel, and this variant is equipped with an internal weapons bay in front of the main landing gear. Recent pictures of the Y-9 ASW variant suggest at least some aircraft have entered operational service.

In December 2017, the Aviation Industry Corporation of China conducted the maiden flight of the AG-600 Kunlong, the world's largest seaplane.[208] The aircraft is still under development, but once operational, the AG-600 probably will be used for both civilian and military roles, such as search and rescue operations or defense needs in the South China Sea. Chinese advertising depicts the aircraft as having an endurance of 12 hours and the capacity to rescue 50 people during a single flight.[209]

Aircraft Carrier Program. In September 2012, China commissioned the *Liaoning*, joining the small group of countries that have an aircraft carrier. Beijing acquired the Soviet ship, formerly the *Varyag*, from Ukraine in 2002.[210,211] Since that time, the PLAN has followed the long and difficult path of learning to operate fixed-wing aircraft from a carrier. The first launches and recoveries of J-15 fighter aircraft occurred in November 2012, with additional testing and training in early July 2013. With the first landing complete, China became only the fifth country in the world to have conventional takeoff and landing fighters aboard an aircraft carrier. In 2017, the *Liaoning* concluded its second deployment to the South China Sea for training—its first with embarked J-15 fighters—and conducted its first port visit to Hong Kong.[212,213,214]

The Aircraft Carrier Liaoning

Image Source: AFP

Length	304.5 meters (999.0 ft)
Beam	70 meters (229.7 ft)
Draft	10.5 meters (34.4 ft)
Flight deck length	304.5 meters (999.0 ft)
Flight deck width	70 meters (229.7 ft)
Flight deck angle	7 degrees
Aircraft launch mechanism	Ski jump
Ski jump angle	14 degrees
Top speed	30 kn (55.6 km/h) (34.5 mph)
Range	3,850 NM (7,130.2 km) (4,430.5 miles) at 29 kn (53.7 km/h) (33.4 mph) 8,500 NM (15,742.0 km) (9,781.6 miles) at 18 kn (33.3 km/h) (20.7 mph)
Crew	1,960
Machinery	8 boilers; 4 turbines; 200,000 shp; 4 shafts
Aircraft	Up to 24 J-15 fighters 6 Z-8 helicopters and 4 Ka-31 helicopters

DEFENSE INTELLIGENCE AGENCY

The *Liaoning's* ski-jump configuration restricts aircraft takeoff weight, limiting maximum ordnance loads and overall combat power. The ski-jump design also means it cannot operate large, specialized support aircraft, such as an AEW aircraft.

China's first carrier air regiment will comprise the Shenyang J-15 Flying Shark. The J-15 is externally similar to the Russian Su-33 Flanker D but has many of the domestic avionics and armament capabilities of the Chinese J-11B Flanker. The J-15 has folding wings, strengthened landing gear, a tailhook under a shortened tail stinger, two-piece slotted flaps, canards, and a retractable inflight-refueling probe on the left side of the nose.

China's aircraft carrier program also includes efforts to develop domestic carriers. In 2017, China launched its first domestic aircraft carrier, which was a modified version of the *Liaoning* and is expected to enter into service by 2019.[215,216] Like the *Liaoning*, the ship lacks catapult capabilities and has a smaller flight deck than U.S. carriers.[217] The PLAN is expected to begin construction in 2018 on its first catapult-capable carrier, which will enable additional fighter aircraft, fixed-wing early warning aircraft, and more rapid flight operations.[218]

Helicopters. The PLAN operates three main helicopter variants: the domestically produced Z-9 and Z-8/Z-18 and the Russian-built Helix. The primary helicopter operated by the PLAN is the Z-9C. In the early 1980s, China obtained a license from France's Aerospatiale (now Air-

Chinese Marines attend an international fleet review.

bus Helicopter) to produce the AS 365N Dauphin II helicopter and its engine. The AS 365s produced in China were labeled as the Z-9, with the naval variant designated Z-9C. The Z-9C is capable of operating from any helicopter-capable PLAN combatant. The Z-9C can be fitted with the KLC-1 search radar and dipping sonar and is usually observed with a single lightweight torpedo. A new roof-mounted EO turret, unguided rockets, and 12.7-mm machinegun pods have been seen on several Z-9Cs during counterpiracy deployments. An upgraded naval version, designated the Z-9D, has been observed carrying small ASCMs.

The Z-8 is also a Chinese-produced helicopter based on a French design. In the late 1970s, the PLAN took delivery of the SA 321 Super Frelon. A reverse-engineered version was designated the Z-8, which reached initial operational capability by 1989. Low-rate production continued through the 1990s and into the early 2000s. The Z-8's size provides a greater cargo

PLAN Z-9 helicopter.

capacity compared with other PLAN helicopters but limits its ability to deploy from most PLAN combatants.

A new PLAN helicopter labeled the Z-18 has operated with the *Liaoning*. The Z-18 comes in three variants: transport, antisubmarine (Z-18F), and AEW (Z-18J). As with the Z-8, the Z-18's size limits its deployment options.

Variants of the Helix are the only imported helicopters operated by the PLAN. In 1999, the PLAN took delivery of an initial batch of eight Russian-built Helix helicopters. Five were Ka-28 Helix As, and three were Helix Ds. An additional 9 Helix As have been delivered, and all 18 Helix are operational. As with the Russian Ka-27s, the exported Ka-28s can perform several mission sets but are usually used for ASW, and the Ka-27PSs are optimized for SAR and logistic support missions. The Ka-28 is fitted with search radar and dipping sonar and can employ sonobuoys, torpedoes, depth charges, or mines.

In 2010, China purchased nine Ka-31 AEW helicopters and its E-801 radar system. The Z-18J and Ka-31 provide the PLAN a serviceable sea-based AEW capability to help fill that critical gap until newer catapult-equipped aircraft carriers capable of operating fixed-wing AEW aircraft enter service.

Training

During the past decade, the scope and frequency of naval training have gradually expanded, reflecting the growing capabilities of China's navy. The PLAN conducts year-round multimission training, including robust antisurface and antiair warfare training.[219] The PLAN now also participates in training exercises farther from China's coasts, in areas such as the western Pacific and the Indian Ocean.

In 2015, *China's Military Strategy* called for the PLA to enhance realistic military training, particularly in complex electromagnetic environments, diverse terrains, and adverse weather conditions.[220] The same year, the PLAN Headquarters Military Training Department directed the PLAN to enhance the complexity of training and exercises by:

- Making training more realistic.

- Strengthening command authority and relationships through realistic opposing force training.

- Deepening tactical innovation.

- Improving training in the actual use of weapons in an electromagnetic environment.

- Continuing "far seas" training.

- Improving training methods by avoiding formalism and scripting in exercises.

- Improving joint campaign-level training.[221]

PLAN participation in missions such as the antipiracy task groups in the Gulf of Aden provide opportunities to train in real-world situations to refine operational capabilities. The Navy also makes use of shore-based simulators and vessel training centers to help maintain year-round readiness levels.[222]

Paramilitary Forces

China Coast Guard. The CCG is responsible for a wide range of missions, including the enforcement of China's sovereignty claims, antismuggling, surveillance, protection of fisheries resources, and general law enforcement. Maritime law enforcement responsibilities before 2013 were scattered across a number of organizations but have since been consolidated to establish more effective command and control. CCG ships are subordinate to the People's Armed Police and take part in Bejing's whole-of-govenrment approach to maritime disputes. China primarily uses civilian maritime law enforcement agencies in maritime disputes, employing the PLAN in a protective capacity in case of escalation.[223]

The CCG has rapidly increased and modernized its forces, improving China's ability to enforce its maritime claims. Since 2010, the CCG's large patrol ship fleet (more than 1,000 tons) has more than doubled in size from about 60 to more than 130 ships, making it by far the largest coast guard force in the world and increasing its capacity to conduct extended offshore operations in a number of disputed areas simultaneously. Furthermore, the newer ships are substantially larger and more capable than the older ships, and the majority are equipped with helicopter facilities, high-capacity water cannons, and guns ranging from 30-mm to 76-mm. Among these ships, a number are capable of long-distance, long-endurance out-of-area operations. In addition, the CCG operates more than 70 fast patrol combatants (more than 500 tons), which can be used for limited offshore operations, and more than 400 coastal patrol craft (as well as about 1,000 inshore and riverine patrol boats). By the end of the decade, the CCG is expected to add up to 30 patrol ships and patrol combatants before the construction program levels off.[224]

Haixun class cutter conducting port visit to Honolulu, Hawaii – September 2012.

Image Source: DVIDS

People's Armed Forces Maritime Militia. The PAFMM is a subset of China's national militia, an armed reserve force of civilians available for mobilization to perform basic support duties. Militia units organize around towns, villages, urban subdistricts, and enterprises, and they vary widely from one location to another. The composition and mission of each unit reflects local conditions and personnel skills. In the South China Sea, the PAFMM plays a major role in coercive activities to achieve China's political goals without fighting, part of broader Chinese military doctrine that states that confrontational operations short of war can be an effective means of accomplishing political objectives.[225]

A large number of PAFMM vessels train with and support the PLA and CCG in tasks such as safeguarding maritime claims, protecting fisheries, and providing logistic support, search and rescue (SAR), and surveillance and reconnaissance. The Chinese government subsidizes local and provincial commercial organizations to operate militia ships to perform "official" missions on an ad hoc basis outside their regular commercial roles. The PAFMM has played a noteworthy role in a number of military campaigns and coercive incidents over the years, including the harassment of Vietnamese survey ships in 2011, a standoff with the Philippines at Scarborough Reef in 2012, and a standoff involving a Chinese oil rig in 2014. In the past, the PAFMM rented fishing boats from companies or individual fisherman, but it appears that China is building a state-owned fishing fleet for its maritime militia force in the South China Sea. Hainan Province, adjacent to the South China Sea, ordered the construction of 84 large militia fishing boats with reinforced hulls and ammunition storage for Sansha City, and the militia took delivery by the end of 2016.[226]

Amphibious Capabilities

The PLAN Marine Corps (PLANMC) is the PLAN's land combat arm. Its primary mission is to conduct offensive and defensive amphibious assault in the South China Sea, including the Paracel Island and Spratly Island chains, and potentially the Senkaku Islands.[227] The PLANMC is tasked with seizing and consolidating beachheads, destroying an opposing force at the beachhead and adjacent areas, organizing landing areas, and supporting landings by the PLAA. Other missions include conducting amphibious raids; seizing and occupying enemy naval bases, seaports, and islands; building beachhead protective zones; and covering the PLAA as it advances inland from the coast.[228]

> The seas and oceans bear on the enduring peace, lasting stability, and sustainable development of China...The traditional mentality that land outweighs the sea must be abandoned.
>
> —Excerpt from *China's Military Strategy*, May 2015

Roles and Missions. The PLANMC's mission appears to be evolving beyond amphibious operations and toward a more expeditionary mission beyond China's borders. This is in line with the PLA's evolving strategy as outlined in *China's Military Strategy*.[229,230] For the PLAN, the New Historic Missions mean an increased focus on "diversified missions" or noncombat missions. Many of the tasks assigned to the armed forces in the white paper are ideally suited to the PLANMC, including ensuring Chinese sovereignty claims, safeguarding China's security and interests "in new domains," safeguarding the security of China's interests overseas, and performing such tasks as emergency rescue and disaster relief, rights and interest protection, and guard duty.[231] The PLANMC already is designated a rapid-reaction force for the PLA and has deployed on numerous occasions in response to natural disasters in China, including floods and earthquakes.[232] The PLANMC is the natural land-based force of choice for HADR efforts overseas. In 2017, the PLA also chose to deploy PLANMC troops to the PLA's first overseas base, in Djibouti, reflecting the Marine Corps' growing role in China's military.

Elements of the PLANMC are consistently deployed as part of the PLAN's counterpiracy task groups operating in the Gulf of Aden.[233] The size of the embarked force is no larger than a platoon. These Marines may be regular infantry troops but more likely come from an amphibious reconnaissance group subordinate to the amphibious reconnaissance battalion. They are highly trained in the tactics, techniques, and

PLA marines conduct helicopter entry/exit training.

procedures required for a counterpiracy mission, including VBSS, hostage rescue, and small-team assault. VBSS tactics include fast-roping or rappelling from PLAN helicopters.[234]

Units. The PLANMC is subordinate to the PLAN and consists of seven brigades.[235] Marine brigades are located in each of the North, East, and South Sea Fleets' areas of responsibility.[236,237] Recent PLA reforms included the establishment of a PLANMC headquarters, probably to oversee the administrative man, train, and equip functions of the growing Marine Corps, and also included the appointment of the PLANMC's first commander.[238,239] Each brigade has a headquarters element, an armored regiment, at least two infantry battalions, a howitzer battalion, a missile battalion, a communications and guard battalion, an engineer and chemical defense battalion, a maintenance battalion, and an amphibious reconnaissance battalion (special operations).[240] Estimates of the PLANMC's troop strength differ widely and have been reported as high as 35,000, but the actual number is

PLANMC units conduct an amphibious assault during a training exercise.

Image Source: AFP

PLANMC Capabilities and Equipment

	ZBD-05 AIFV	ZLT-05 AAG	PLZ-07B SP Howitzer
Weight	26.5 tons	28 tons	24.5 tons
Crew	3 + 8 infantry	4	5
Speed (in water)	~20 kn	~20 kn	UNK
Speed (on land)	+40 mph	+40 mph	+40 mph
Main armament	30-mm cannon (4-km max range)	105-mm gun	122-mm cannon (18-km max range)
	Red Arrow antitank guided missile (ATGM)(2x)	Red Arrow ATGM	

probably between 28,000 and 35,000, evenly divided among the 7 brigades.[241,242,243] The PLAN provides the PLANMC with both maritime and air (helicopter) transport, a force enabler for PLANMC amphibious warfare operations.[244] The PLANMC does not have an organic air assault element and probably would rely on PLAN ground-attack fixed-wing aircraft or PLAA helicopters in a close air support role. The PLANMC also has a limited logistics capability.

Equipment. The PLANMC is a fully amphibious force capable of conducting amphibious assault operations using combined-arms tactics and multiple avenues of approach. It is the most capable amphibious force of any South China Sea claimant. The PLANMC can simultaneously seize multiple islands in the Spratlys. It also is capable of rapidly reinforcing China's outposts in the Paracels. The PLANMC still faces challenges and limitations in close air support/air assault and logistics sustainment for large-scale amphibious operations. The PLANMC is incapable of defeating near-peer or peer countries such as the United States, Japan, South Korea, and Russia in amphibious or ground warfare.

The PLANMC's primary fighting vehicles are based on a single chassis and include the ZBD-05 AIFV and the ZLT-05 amphibious assault gun.[245,246] Noncombatant amphibious variants of the ZBD chassis include an armored recovery vehicle and an armored ambulance.[247] Additional combat equipment includes man-portable air defense systems, antipersonnel mortars, antitank rocket launchers, and flamethrowers. The PLANMC is also equipped with amphibious combat engineering equipment for obstacle removal, beach improvement, and construction of defenses once ashore.[248]

APPENDIX C: PLA Air Force

The PLAAF is the largest air force in the region and the third largest in the world, with more than 2,500 total aircraft (not including UAVs or trainers) and 1,700 combat aircraft (including fighters, strategic bombers, tactical bombers, and multimission tactical and attack aircraft). The PLAAF is closing the gap with Western air forces across a broad spectrum of capabilities, such as aircraft performance, C2, and electronic warfare.

In 2017, the PLAAF reorganized its force structure as part of broader PLA reforms. Changes included establishing at least six new airbases and restructuring the force's previously subordinate regiments into brigades under these newly established bases by disbanding fighter and fighter-bomber divisions. The PLAAF also relocated or resubordinated some units to different theater commands and redesignated the 15th Airborne Corps as the PLA Airborne Corps. [249]

Roles and Missions

The PLAAF's role is to serve as a comprehensive strategic air force capable of long-range airpower projection:[250]

> In line with the strategic requirement of building air-space capabilities and conducting offensive and defensive operations, the PLA Air Force (PLAAF) will endeavor to shift its focus from territorial air defense to both defense and offense and build an air-space defense force structure that can meet the requirements of informatized operations. The PLAAF will boost its capabilities for strategic early warning, air strike, air and missile defense, information countermeasures, airborne operations, strategic projection, and comprehensive support.
>
> —Excerpt from *China's Military Strategy*, May 2015

The above excerpt illustrates the expanding roles and missions of the PLAAF. Whereas in the mid-1990s, the PLAAF's primary responsibilities were to protect China's airfields, urban centers, transportation systems, and military facilities, the PLAAF is enhancing its ability to conduct both offensive and defensive air operations farther from China's borders.[251]

DEFENSE INTELLIGENCE AGENCY

Major Air Units

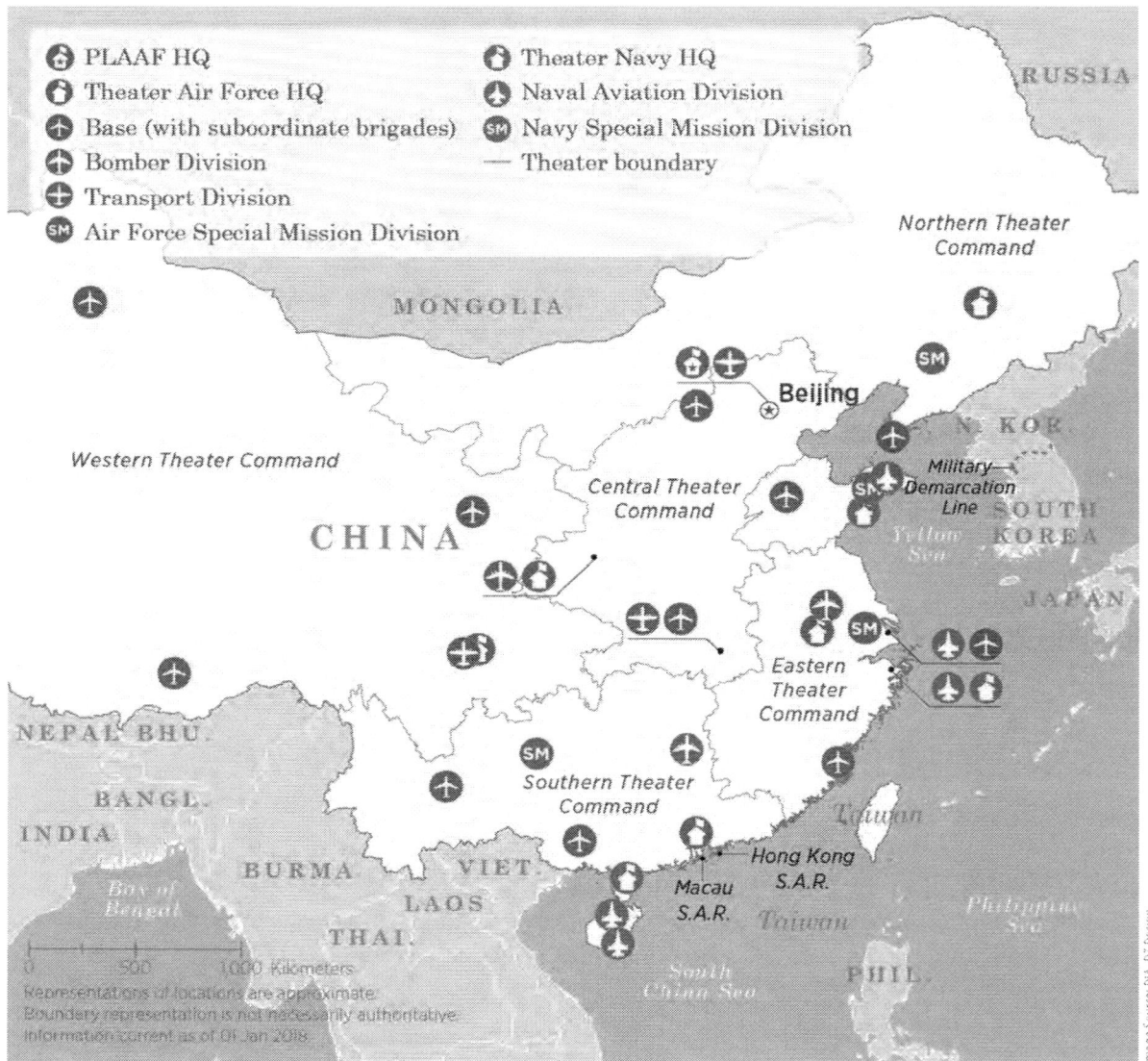

Legend:
- PLAAF HQ
- Theater Air Force HQ
- Base (with subordinate brigades)
- Bomber Division
- Transport Division
- Air Force Special Mission Division
- Theater Navy HQ
- Naval Aviation Division
- Navy Special Mission Division
- — Theater boundary

Northern Theater Command

Western Theater Command

Central Theater Command

Eastern Theater Command

Southern Theater Command

Military Demarcation Line

Beijing

MONGOLIA

RUSSIA

N. KOR.

SOUTH KOREA

JAPAN

CHINA

Yellow Sea

Taiwan

NEPAL BHU.

BANGL.

INDIA

Bay of Bengal

BURMA

LAOS

THAI.

VIET.

Hong Kong S.A.R.

Macau S.A.R.

South China Sea

Taiwan

Philippine Sea

PHIL.

0   500   1000 Kilometers

Representations of locations are approximate.
Boundary representation is not necessarily authoritative.
Information current as of 01 Jan 2018.

Equipment

Bombers. China's bomber force comprises variants of the H-6 Badger bomber, and the PLAAF has worked to maintain and enhance the operational effectiveness of these aircraft. The H-6K variant, which China is fielding in greater numbers, integrates standoff weapons and features more efficient turbofan engines in redesigned wing roots.[252] This extended-range aircraft can carry six LACMs, providing the PLA a long-range, standoff, precision-strike capability that can reach Guam.

The PLAAF is developing new medium- and long-range stealth bombers to strike regional and global targets. Stealth technology continues to play a key role in the development of these new bombers, which probably will reach initial operational capability no sooner than 2025. These new bombers will have additional capabilities, with full-spectrum upgrades compared with current operational bomber fleets, and will employ many fifth-generation fighter technologies in their design.

Early Warning. Airborne early warning and control (AEW&C) aircraft, such as China's KJ-2000 Mainring, KJ-200 Moth, and KJ-500, are force multipliers, amplifying the capabilities to detect, track, and target threats. These aircraft extend the range of a country's integrated air defense system network. In particular, these systems are better suited to detecting low-altitude targets at greater standoff distances.

PLAAF AEW&C aircraft also incorporate state-of-the-art radar technology, such as active electronically scanned array radars that offer instantaneous target updates, electronic beam steering, advanced/specialized radar modes, very large search volumes, and the ability to stare at a target or track thousands of targets simultaneously. These features combine to provide faster target acquisition time, more accurate target position data, and increased ability to detect low-observable targets.

PLAAF J-11BS multirole fighter aircraft.

Image Source: AFP

Fighters. Although the PLAAF still operates a large number of older second- and third-generation fighters, it will probably become a majority fourth-generation force within the next several years. The PLAAF has fielded at least 600 fourth-generation fighters and is already developing fifth-generation fighters. *[Note: what the U.S. and Western militaries refer to as fourth-generation fighters, China refers to as third-generation. This is because the PLA never had first-generation fighters—its first fighter aircraft were second-generation fighters acquired from Russia.]*

Fourth-generation fighter aircraft*—which include the Chinese J-10B/C, J-11B, and J-16—are generally characterized by the following:

- Electronically or mechanically scanned multimode radars, passive infrared search and track systems.
- "Glass" cockpits with multifunction displays (MFDs), improved heads-up display (HUD), and helmet-mounted sight (HMS).
- High-bandwidth communications and datalinks and identification, friend or foe (IFF).
- Advanced electronic warfare (EW) avionics, including digital jamming system, radar warning receiver, chaff/flare dispensers, and adaptive countermeasures.
- Engines with increased thrust and service life; advanced weapons, including long-range air-to-air missiles (AAMs), off-boresight short-range AAMs, LACMs, ASCMs, and precision-guided munitions (PGMs).
- Passive electronically scanned array or active electronically scanned array (AESA) radars. These radars provide long-range radar detection and electronically scanned radar beams that enable automatic target acquisition, tracking of multiple targets, and highly accurate targeting data for air-to-air and precision air-to-ground engagements.
- Digital radiofrequency memory (DRFM) jammers enabling instantaneous smart jamming responses by automatically selecting jamming waveforms to counter a specific radar threat—significantly improving fighter aircraft survivability.

Fifth-generation fighter aircraft*, including the developmental Chinese J-20 and FC-31/J-31, are commonly defined by the following state-of-the-art technologies:

- Stealthy aircraft designs with significantly reduced radar and infrared signatures.
- AESA radars.
- Long-range, multiband EO targeting systems.
- Sensor fusion.
- Advanced glass cockpits with large MFDs and HMSs.
- Advanced datalinks fusing data from air and ground networks.
- Internal carriage of off-boresight and long-range AAMs, LACMs, ASCMs, and PGMs.
- Sophisticated EW suites with advanced DRFM jammers and EO defensive systems.
- Super maneuverability and/or super cruise capability (ability to fly above Mach 1 without use of afterburner).
- Designed with network-centric warfare technology; will have potent air-to-air lethality and standoff attack capabilities in sensor-to-shooter operations.

*U.S.- defined fourth and fifth generation fighter aircraft in China.

PLAAF KJ-2000 airborne early warning and control system aircraft.

Image Source: AFP

Unmanned Aerial Vehicles. During the past 2 years, the PLA has improved its UAV capabilities, unveiled new aircraft that combine strike capability with aerial reconnaissance, and deployed select platforms to new areas, such as the South China Sea. Examples include China's first turbine-powered armed reconnaissance UAV, the Yunying (Cloud Shadow), and the armed ISR UAV Gongji 1. China also has sold armed UAVs to customers such as Iraq. Marketing material for China's armed UAVs cites speeds of 170 mph, endurance of 20 hours, and payloads of two or more air-to-surface guided munitions.

Surface-to-Air Missiles. The PLAAF has one of the largest forces of advanced long-range SAM systems in the world, made up of a combination of Russian-sourced SA-20 (S-300PMU1/2) battalions and domestically produced CSA-9 (HQ-9) battalions. In early

2018, Russia began delivering to China the S-400/Triumf SAM system, which Beijing will use to improve its strategic air defense systems as a follow-on to the SA-20.[253] The PLAAF may simultaneously develop its domestically produced CSA-X-19 (HQ-19) to provide the basis for a ballistic missile defense capability.

Transport. China's aviation industry continues to test its Y-20 large transport aircraft for introduction into the PLA's operational inventory to supplement and eventually replace China's small fleet of strategic airlift assets, which includes a limited number of Russian-made Il-76 aircraft. The Y-20 conducted its maiden flight in early 2013 and reportedly uses the same Russian engines as the Il-76. The large transports are intended to support airborne C2, logistics, paradrop, aerial refueling, and strategic reconnaissance operations as well as HADR.

Effective use of information is critical to strengthening the PLAAF, and development and acquisition of systems and platforms are trending in this direction. Information demand will necessitate a tight synchronization of C4ISR with operations. By 2020, the PLAAF probably hopes to develop an ISR capability to effectively support traditional air missions, including ground support and air superiority, along with the PLA's emerging military capabilities in space. From the PLAAF's perspective, this essentially means seamlessly melding all of its air and space capabilities, a significant challenge.

Aircraft Systems Characteristics

Chinese Manned Aircraft	U.S. Generation	Mission/Role	Status	AESA Radar	Long-Range A/A Missiles	Off-Bore-sight A/A Missiles	Precision-Guided Munitions	Speed
J-7	2nd	Fighter	Operational					Mach 2 class
J-8	3rd	Fighter	Operational		X			Mach 2 class
Su-30	4th	Multirole Fighter	Operational		X	X	X	Mach 2 class
J-10A	4th	Multirole Fighter	Operational				X	Mach 1.8 class
J-11B	4th	Multirole Fighter	Operational		X	X		Mach 2 class
J-10B	4th+	Multirole Fighter	Operational		X	X	X	Mach 1.8 class
J-10C	4th+	Multirole Fighter		X	X	X	X	Mach 1.8 class
J-16	4th+	Multirole Fighter		X	X	X	X	Mach 2 class
Su-35S	4th+	Multirole Fighter	Buying from Russia		X	X	X	Mach 2 class
J-20	5th	Multirole Fighter	Development	X	X	X	X	Mach 2 class
FC-31/J-31	5th	Multirole Fighter	Development	X	X	X	X	Mach 1.8 class
JH-7	N/A	Fighter-Bomber	Operational				X	Mach 1.7 class
H-6	N/A	Bomber	Operational				X	Subsonic
Tactical Bomber	Next Gen	Fighter-Bomber	Development	X	X		X	
Strategic Bomber	Next Gen	Long-Range Bomber	Development	X			X	
KJ-2000	N/A	AEW&C	Operational	X				Subsonic
KJ-200	N/A	AEW&C	Operational	X				Subsonic
KJ-500	N/A	AEW&C	Operational	X				Subsonic

+ Indicates a generation of aircraft has been partially upgraded with next-generation capabilities.

PLAAF literature paints a detailed picture of tomorrow's air wars battlespace. It will be an uncertain, hotly contested environment where decisions will be made with extreme alacrity, requiring highly specialized equipment. The entire battlespace will be information-driven, from command staff decisions and supporting C2 all the way to the very weapons the PLAAF desires.

Two J-10 fighters refueling with an H-6U tanker.

Image Source: AFP

Airborne Corps. As part of ongoing military reforms, in 2017 the PLAAF reorganized its airborne units into a new corps—the PLA Airborne Corps—consisting of six airborne brigades, a special operations brigade, an aviation brigade, and a support brigade. Previously, airborne forces fell under the PLAAF 15th Airborne Corps and were organized into three airborne divisions, supported by a special operations group, with both fixed- and rotary-wing assets.[254] The PLA Airborne Corps' main purpose is to carry out operations including parachute, aircraft landing, and mixed parachute and aircraft landing. According to PLAA doctrine, the main advantage of airborne operations is to "cut across ground defense lines and topographical obstacles to unfold attacks directly inside the enemy disposition."[255] These operations are designed to support main-force operational efforts, seize and hold key targets and areas in the enemy's depth (such as airfields and bridges), block an enemy's retreat, block reinforcement by enemy reserve forces, and conduct raids on key targets in the enemy's depth.[256]

Training and Exercises

Numerous professional articles and speeches by high-ranking Chinese officers indicate the PLAAF does not believe that its past training practices prepared its pilots and other personnel for actual combat. Unrealistic training manifested itself in multiple ways that hindered the PLA's air combat capabilities. The PLA recognizes that a gap exists between the skills of its pilots and those in "the air forces of powerful nations." To address training weaknesses, the former PLAAF commander said that when the PLAAF trains, it must "train for battle" instead of "doing things for show…[or] going through the motions."

During the past few years, the PLAAF has revamped its training program and now seeks to replicate real-world combat environments as closely as possible. Through its four "name-brand exercises"—RED SWORD, GOLDEN HELMET, GOLDEN DART, and BLUE SHIELD—the PLAAF is making incremental improvements to its training regimen. The PLAAF continues to seek engagement with foreign air forces, such as by participating in the Russian-sponsored Aviadarts air-to-ground competition and the FALCON STRIKE exercise with the Royal Thai Air Force, to gain exposure to foreign operational concepts and tactics.

The effect of these training initiatives on operational capabilities remains to be seen; however, the PLAAF is beginning to codify fundamental changes to the training philosophy that are expected to improve the PLA's air capabilities during the coming years. A key factor in this development is the PLAAF's use of advanced air combat maneuvering instrumentation (ACMI) systems, which enable the force to train with more realism and learn more from each event while meeting safety requirements. The ACMI system allows the PLAAF to monitor air combat training in real time and to adjudicate interactions such as aircraft maneuvering, weapons employment, jamming, and use of chaff and flares. Coupled with foreign engagements, the use of ACMI in training offers the PLAAF the opportunity to accelerate its progress in training.

The PLAAF has also made advances in joint training. Traditionally Army-only exercises now incorporate PLAAF participation, and large-scale joint exercises have given the PLA opportunities to test its forces' progress toward being able to operate in a true joint environment. Although more recent exercises suggest improvement and increased sophistication, systemic shortfalls identified in several PLA training events—difficulty in coordination, obstacles to information sharing, limited realism, and a continued reliance on scripting—persist as problems for PLA and PLAAF leaders, hampering key functions, such as air defense, targeting, battle damage assessment, and air support to ground forces.

Two fighter jets during a military drill over the South China Sea.

APPENDIX D: PLA Rocket Force

As part of military reforms initiated in late 2015, the PLA Second Artillery Force was renamed the PLA Rocket Force (PLARF), and for the first time the force was elevated to a full service on equal footing with the PLA Army, Navy, and Air Force. PLARF weapons systems include dozens of ICBMs and hundreds of theater-range missiles for precision strike against major adversary military and civilian infrastructure.[257]

Roles and Missions

The PLARF operates China's strategic land-based nuclear and conventional missiles and is a critical component of China's deterrence strategy and efforts to counter third-party intervention in regional conflicts. The PLARF also is charged with developing and testing several new classes and variants of long-range missiles, forming additional missile units, upgrading older missile systems, and developing methods to counter ballistic missile defenses.

Principal Weapon Systems

The PLARF has about 1,200 short-range ballistic missiles (SRBMs), and China is increasing the lethality of its conventional missile force by fielding the CSS-11/DF-16 ballistic missile, with a range of 800 to 1,000 kilometers. The CSS-11/DF-16, coupled with the already deployed conventional land-attack and antiship variants of the CSS-5/DF-21

medium-range ballistic missile (MRBM), will improve China's ability to strike not only Taiwan but other regional targets.

The Rocket Force is fielding conventional MRBMs to increase the range at which it can conduct precision strikes against land targets and naval ships (including aircraft carriers) operating from China's shores out to the first island chain—the islands running from the Kurils, through Taiwan, to Borneo, roughly encompassing the Yellow Sea, East China Sea, and South China Sea. The CSS-5 Mod-5/DF-21D has a range exceeding 1,500 kilometers and has a maneuverable warhead. During the PLA's 90th anniversary parade in 2017, China displayed a new MRBM designated the DF-16G, which China claims features high accuracy, short preparation time, and an improved maneuverable terminal stage that can better infiltrate missile defense systems.[258]

China unveiled the DF-26 intermediate-range ballistic missile (IRBM) during its September 2015 military parade in Beijing. The DF-26 is capable of conducting precision strikes against ground targets and contributes to China's counterintervention posture in the Asia-Pacific region. During the parade, official public statements also referenced a nuclear version of the DF-26, which, if it has the same guidance capabilities, would give China its first nuclear precision-strike capability against theater targets.

A CSS-5 Mod 5/DF-21D antiship ballistic missile (ASBM) system on parade.

The PLARF also continues to enhance its nuclear deterrent, maintaining silo-based nuclear ICBMs and adding more survivable, mobile nuclear delivery systems. China currently has 75 to 100 ICBMs, including the silo-based CSS-4 Mod 2/DF-5A and MIRV-equipped CSS-4 Mod 3/DF-5B; the solid-fueled, road-mobile CSS-10 Mod 1/DF-31 and CSS-10 Mod 2/DF-31A; and the shorter range CSS-3/DF-4. The CSS-10 Mod 2/DF-31A has a range of more than 11,200 kilometers and can reach most locations within the continental United States. China also is developing a new MIRV-capable road-mobile ICBM, the CSS-X-10/DF-41.

The CJ-10 ground-launched cruise missile (GLCM) has a range in excess of 1,500 kilometers and offers flight profiles different from ballistic missiles, enhancing targeting options. Because of overlap in the kinds of targets China is likely to engage with either ballistic missiles or cruise missiles, GLCMs and air-launched land-attack cruise missiles provide key operational and planning flexibility. These weapons are likely to reduce the burden on ballistic missile forces as well as create somewhat safer strike opportunities for Chinese aircrews, allowing them to engage from much greater distances and from more advantageous locations. This will complicate an adversary's air and missile defense problem.

PLA Rocket Force Systems*

System	Type	Warheads	Propellant	Deployment Mode	Max Range km
CSS-3/DF-4	ICBM	Nuclear	Liquid	ROTL**	5,500+
CSS-4/DF-5	ICBM	Nuclear	Liquid	Silo	12,000-13,000
CSS-7/DF-11	SRBM	Conventional	Solid	Mobile	300-600
CSS-6/DF-15	SRBM	Conventional	Solid	Mobile	600-850+
CSS-11/DF-16	SRBM	Conventional	Solid	Mobile	800-1,000
CSS-5/DF-21	MRBM	Nuclear and Conventional Variants	Solid	Mobile	1,500-1,750+
CSS-5 Mod-5/DF-21D	ASBM	Conventional	Solid	Mobile	1,500+
DF-26	IRBM	Nuclear and Conventional Variants	Solid	Mobile	4,000
CSS-10/DF-31	ICBM	Nuclear	Solid	Mobile	7,200-11,200
CJ-10	GLCM	Conventional	Solid	Mobile	1500+

*This chart does not include systems in development.

** Rollout to Launch

China's Conventional and Nuclear Strike Range

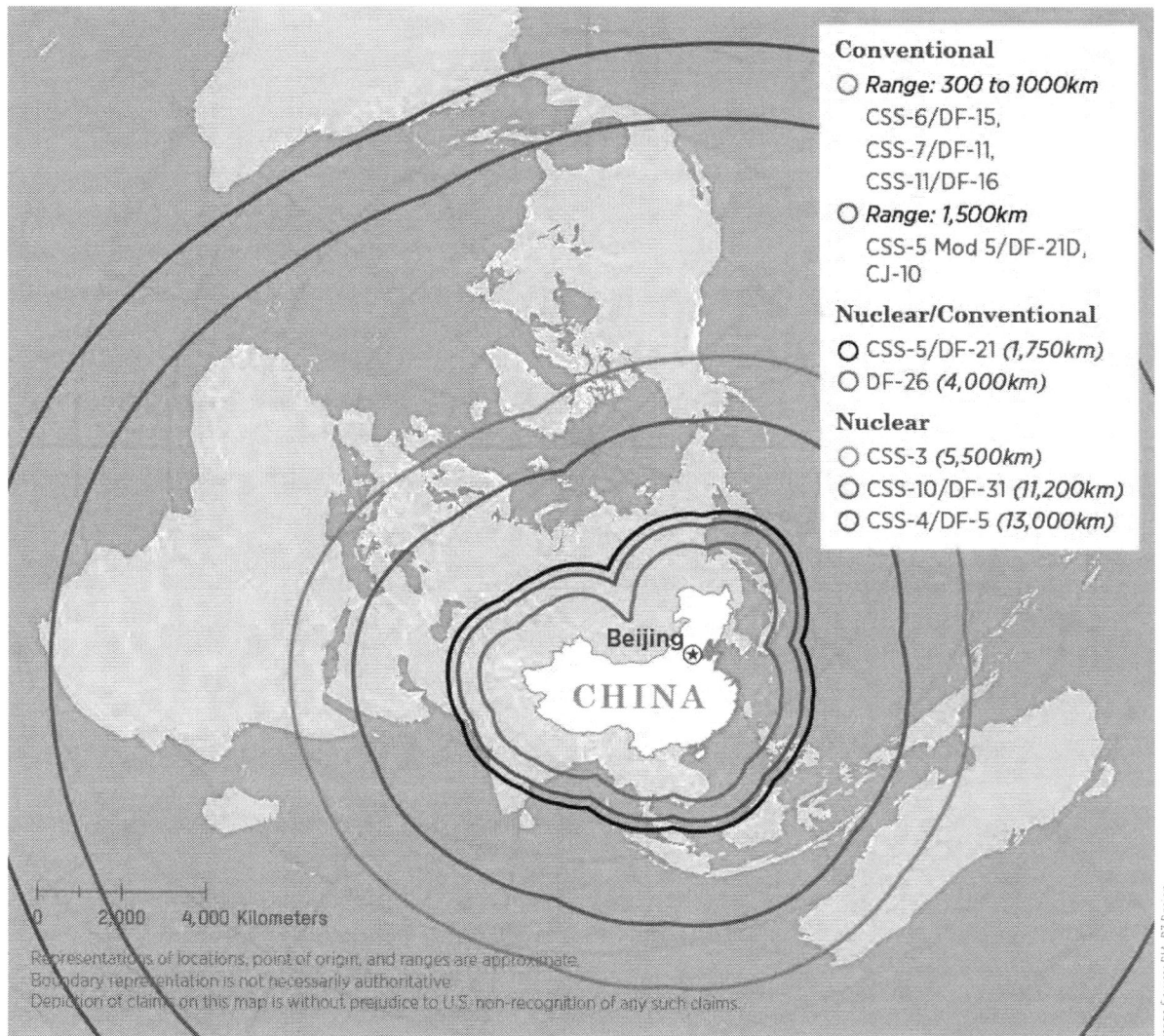

Conventional
- ○ *Range: 300 to 1000km*
  CSS-6/DF-15,
  CSS-7/DF-11,
  CSS-11/DF-16
- ○ *Range: 1,500km*
  CSS-5 Mod 5/DF-21D,
  CJ-10

Nuclear/Conventional
- ○ CSS-5/DF-21 *(1,750km)*
- ○ DF-26 *(4,000km)*

Nuclear
- ○ CSS-3 *(5,500km)*
- ○ CSS-10/DF-31 *(11,200km)*
- ○ CSS-4/DF-5 *(13,000km)*

Beijing

CHINA

0   2,000   4,000 Kilometers

Representations of locations, point of origin, and ranges are approximate.
Boundary representation is not necessarily authoritative.
Depiction of claims on this map is without prejudice to U.S. non-recognition of any such claims.

Image Source: DIA, D3 Design

CHINA MILITARY POWER | *Modernizing a Force to Fight and Win*

Training

PLARF participation in joint force training has increased during the past few years, and all PLA joint training events probably now include at least some level of PLARF involvement, such as PLARF field operations in support of the exercise. This development indicates an increased emphasis on joint firepower operations.

The PLARF is moving away from a dependence on conscripted personnel and is developing a technically qualified enlisted force. In addition, the force is modifying its annual training cycle to incorporate more complicated training earlier in the year, enabling PLARF units to better prepare to participate in PLA joint training in the fall. The force also reportedly has implemented a rating system for unit training as well as accreditation criteria for personnel at critical posts.

The PLARF now regularly conducts training under extreme weather and geographical conditions and in complex electromagnetic and nuclear, biological, and chemical environments. The PLARF's goal is to train under actual combat conditions, which include contending with enemy special forces, satellite reconnaissance, electromagnetic jamming, and air attacks. To that end, the PLARF has worked to improve its training against a modern (informatized) "blue force" that portrays a superior adversary.

PLARF training includes annual live missile launches that allow the missile brigades to practice all required procedures. Much like the increase in complexity for other PLA training events, recent Rocket Force guidance has called for the participating missile units to increase the difficulty and intensity of live launches.

DEFENSE INTELLIGENCE AGENCY

APPENDIX E: PLA Strategic Support Force

Strategic Support Force Insignia

Image Source: Wikicommons

In December 2015, Beijing established the Strategic Support Force (SSF) to provide the PLA with cyber, aerospace, and electronic warfare capabilities.[259] The SSF forms the core of China's information warfare force, supports the entire PLA, and reports directly to the CMC. The force's formation appears to be the outcome of debate in the PLA since the 1980s regarding PLA needs in a potential conflict with peer nations. According to a Ministry of National Defense spokesman, "The SSF will integrate reconnaissance, early warning, communications, command, control, [and] navigation … and will provide strong support for joint operations for each military service branch."[260]

A key aspect of the SSF is that the new body unites previously dispersed elements, pro-

viding more centralized command and control of China's cyber, space, and electronic warfare capabilities. Before the 2015 structural reforms, for example, responsibility for space, cyber, and electronic warfare missions rested with offices across the former General Armaments Department and the General Staff Department (GSD), including the GSD Technical Department and GSD Electronic Countermeasures and Radar Department.

The SSF constitutes the first steps in the development of a cyberforce by combining cyber reconnaissance, cyberattack, and cyberdefense capabilities into one organization to reduce bureaucratic hurdles and centralize command and control. The SSF also appears to be in line with PLA efforts to support and execute modern informatized warfare.

The PLA's 90th anniversary parade in July 2017 included the participation of an SSF electronic reconnaissance formation, which reportedly provides highly mobile, integrated, flexible, multidomain information warfare capabilities. The unit's mission reportedly is seizing and maintaining battlefield information control. This focus on the SSF and one of its premier units suggests that the PLA is increasing the priority and prominence of the SSF and its assigned missions to tackle the military's deficiencies in controlling complex electromagnetic environments.[261]

APPENDIX F: *Chinese Intelligence Services*

In June 2017, China passed a National Intelligence Law specifying that "state intelligence work" would fall under the "central national security leadership body," and military intelligence work would fall under the Central Military Commission.[262] The central national security leadership body may refer to an intelligence committee structure subordinate to China's Central National Security Commission.[263] The PLA's national-level intelligence system is still undergoing changes as part of broader military reform efforts.

Civilian Intelligence. The Ministry of State Security (MSS) is China's main civilian intelligence and counterintelligence service.[264] MSS missions include protecting China's national security, securing political and social stability, implementing the updated State Security Law and related laws and regulations, protecting state secrets, and conducting counterintelligence.[265]

Domestic Security. The Ministry of Public Security (MPS) is China's principal domestic security agency and is responsible for overseeing the country's domestic policing and public security activities. Although the MPS is not directly involved in domestic intelligence gathering, it has domestic intelligence functions, including investigating corruption cases, countering threats to political and social stability, countering terrorism, and policing the Internet.[266,267]

Political Work. The General Political Department Liaison Department, which probably was renamed the Political Work Department Liaison Bureau (PWD/LB) during recent reforms, is the PLA's principal organization responsible for political warfare and for collecting and analyzing intelligence information regarding senior-level officers from the United States, Taiwan, Japan, and other defense establishments of interest.[268][269] The PWD/LB functions as an interlocking directorate that operates at the nexus of politics, finance, military operations, and intelligence. The PWD/LB has few analogous counterparts in modern democratic societies.[270]

Military Intelligence. The former PLA Second Department (2PLA) was a subdepartment of the GSD. Postreform, the 2PLA has been identified as the Intelligence Bureau of the Joint Staff Department under the Central Military Commission.[271] This bureau carries out the military's overt reporting and clandestine human intelligence collection operations, provides indications and warning and other analysis to the CMC leadership, runs the defense attaché network, and manages intelligence produced by dedicated PLA reconnaissance assets.[272,273,274]

Signals Intelligence. The former PLA Third Department (3PLA) was one of the GSD's subdepartments but postreform has probably been renamed and subordinated under the SSF. This element controls a vast signals intelligence (SIGINT) and computer network operations infrastructure. The PLA's SIGINT and cyber assets target foreign satellite, line of sight, and over-the-horizon communications, as well as computer networks.[275,276]

Electronic Intelligence. The former PLA Fourth Department (4PLA) was a subdepartment of the GSD, but postreform has probably been renamed and subordinated to the SSF. This element is primarily responsible for offensive electronic warfare, but it is generally believed to maintain electronic intelligence capabilities.[277,278]

APPENDIX G: Military Resources, Infrastructure, and Logistics

The PLA's centralized control supply system uses a push-pull process for replenishment. This means that supplies are pushed to the troops based on standard demand and use; individual units pull supplies when they require additional materiel. Shortfalls in logistic support to PLA operations, even going back to China's military conflict with Vietnam in the late 1970s, when troops were ill equipped and encountered replenishment problems, have prompted the PLA to modernize its logistic support to match the modern requirements of its forces.[279] This incremental transformation began in 2002 but also has been a major focus of the PLA's ongoing reform efforts.

The PLA has gradually integrated its military and civilian sectors by drawing on private (or civilian) companies to supplement its logistics resources. Before reforms, the PLA's supply system was controlled at multiple levels. The former General Logistics Department (GLD) provided general purpose supplies, such as food, shelter, and fuel. Specific branches of each service maintained special materiel unique to the PLAN and PLAAF. Redundant service and joint supply processes created inefficiencies within the logistics system. Corruption, bribery, and misuse of funds further reduced the effectiveness of strategic logistic support. Reforms to the PLA logistics system combined with vigorous anticorruption measures are intended to both improve the efficiency of logistic support and reduce waste within the system.[280,281]

PLAN Fusu class replenishment ship *Qinghaihu.*

Image Source: DVIDS

As part of the 2015 reorganization, the CMC eliminated the GLD, replacing the organization with the Logistic Support Department (LSD). The new LSD's strategic and administrative roles include establishing logistic policies and conducting inspections.[282] The LSD also provides oversight for the general purpose supply chain, military facility construction, and equipment management. The head of the LSD does not have a seat on the CMC, unlike his predecessor in the GLD, probably in part to reduce corruption and streamline PLA command and control.

Separately, the PLA established the Joint Logistic Support Force (JLSF) in September 2016, charged with planning and executing integrated joint logistic support for strategic campaign operations.[283,284] The JLSF oversees theaterwide supply operations, while service branches retain service-specific supply responsibilities.[285] The force is headquartered at a joint logistic support base in Wuhan and commands five subordinate support centers.[286] The reorganization centralizes logistics operations under one chain of command to more efficiently support theater and strategic logistics operations.

Much like structural changes that separated operational control of the PLA from force-building efforts among the PLA's services, the establishment of the LSD and JLSF separated logistics management from logistic support to combat operations and probably was intended to shorten resource replenishment timelines across the PLA. These logistic reforms require testing to determine whether they will be effective in helping China overcome some of its combat inefficiencies and successfully support regional and national military operations.

> [The PLA will focus on] developing uniform military and civilian standards for infrastructure, key technical areas, and major industries, exploring methods for training military personnel in industries, and outsourcing logistics support to civilian support systems.
>
> —Excerpt from *China's Military Strategy*, May 2015

The PLA also has continued its efforts to improve civil-military integration as a core function of logistic support to military operations under the LSD and JLSF constructs. This entails leveraging civilian sector capabilities and technologies to support military logistics to improve efficiency and reduce costs.

The PLA continues to increase its use of civilian-controlled assets in military operations and exercises, most notably civilian ground transportation and ships supporting joint exercises and civilian firms providing supplies to mitigate logistic shortfalls.[287,288,289]

Military Transportation

China has a robust transportation infrastructure and is enlarging its transportation network to keep up with the country's economic growth and increasing military demand. Although most of China's rail lines, roads, and seaports are sufficient to support military transportation and mobilization, the variability of infrastructure throughout the country is an ongoing challenge. For example, western China's transportation network is more limited than that of eastern China.[290,291,292] Beijing is addressing this problem by initiating infrastructure projects and targeted funding allocations. Future transportation network improvements will bolster the PLA's ability to mobilize by moving higher numbers of units more expediently across greater spans of the country.

The PLA primarily relies on rail transport to move large numbers of ground troops and large amounts of equipment.[293] The Chinese rail network comprises about 100,000 kilometers of rail, 10,000 kilometers of which is high-speed track supporting trains running at up to 250 kilometers per hour.[294] The PLA also relies on the road network to transport troops and military equipment. Traffic congestion, tolls, and bottlenecks limit the capacity of eastern

China's expressways in major cities.[295] Road conditions vary from good to poorly maintained in rural areas, restricting capacity and increasing travel times.[296,297] China expects to build about 1.3 million kilometers of roads and 26,000 kilometers of expressways by 2020.[298]

China also is improving its existing domestic airfields to handle heavier payloads, constructing airfields on islands and outposts in the South China Sea, and restructuring airfields to support military and civilian use.[299] As of June 2016, about one-third of China's airports supported military and civilian use.[300] The PLA exercises control of China's airspace, filling a role similar to that which the Federal Aviation Administration plays in controlling airspace in the United States. Although the Civil Aviation Administration of China administers Chinese civil aviation, PLA authority takes precedence over the airspace. Consequently, the PLA regularly adjusts civil aviation schedules and flightpaths to avoid PLA activities, such as exercises and other operations.

In mid-2016, China allocated $600 billion as part of a 3-year plan (2016-2018) to continue improving its transportation network and, later the same year, passed the Defense Transportation Law (DTL) authorizing the management, development, and production of dual-use facilities and equipment to support national and regional PLA operations.[301] The DTL also regulates the planning, construction, management, and use of transportation resources for national defense.[302] Governments above the county level are required to include national defense transportation development in their socioeconomic development plan and to give the military basic information about civil transportation tools.[303] The DTL grants the PLA authority over civil transportation systems during wartime. Structuring the transportation infrastructure and facilities as a dual-use system avoids the additional costs of building separate airports, railways, ports, and roads for the military. The PLA's efforts to obtain access to commercial ports in Africa, the Middle East, and South Asia would align with its future overseas logistic needs and meet its evolving naval requirements. The PLAN is likely to use commercial ports and civilian ships to support its international and domestic logistic operations, resupply, replenishment, and maintenance.

China's territorial claims in the South China Sea are driving major logistic developments in the Spratly and Paracel Islands. China's reclaimed territory in the South China Sea is equipped with harbors and berthing areas that are capable of accommodating large naval ships, increasing the PLAN's ability to exercise control of critical SLOCs.[304]

China is expanding its access to foreign ports, such as in Gwadar, Pakistan, to pre-position the logistic framework necessary to support the PLA's growing presence abroad, including normalizing and sustaining deployments into and beyond the Indian Ocean. China's announcement in 2015 of its intention to build military facilities in Djibouti cited aims "to help the Navy and Army further participate in UN peacekeeping operations, carry out escort missions in the waters near Somalia and the Gulf of Aden, and provide humanitarian assistance."

China's Outposts in the Spratly Islands

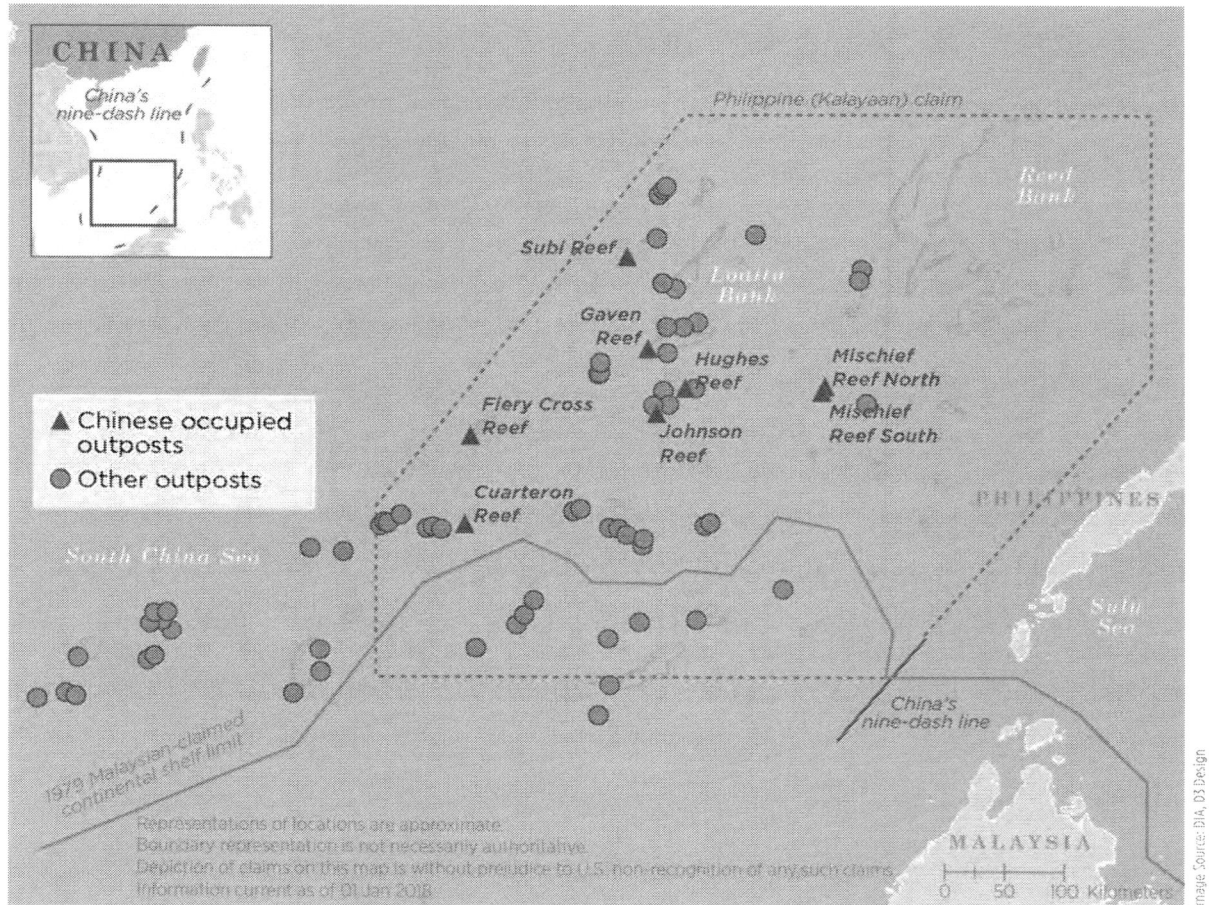

China's claims in the Spratly Islands require constant resupply from the mainland.

Transportation is also at the heart of the Belt and Road Initiative (BRI), which consists of establishing roads, railways, and ports to connect to countries from Asia to Africa and Europe. Although the BRI is marketed as primarily an effort to increase trade and development, China's improved domestic transportation infrastructure and access to transportation infrastructure abroad also would benefit the PLA by enhancing PLA access to transportation hubs and road systems.[305,306,307]

APPENDIX H: *Defense Industry*

Defense Industry Reform

China's defense-industrial complex continues to adapt and reorganize in an effort to improve weapon system research, development, and production to compensate for an estimated lag of one to two generations behind its main competitors in the global arms industry. Over the past 2 years, China has undertaken organizational and policy measures to reenergize the military's work on defense research and innovation through cooperation with the market sector.

- In 2016, the CMC established the Science and Technology Commission, a high-level defense research body, as an independent organization under the high command. It also emphasized the importance of "civil-military integration," a phrase used in part to refer to the leveraging of dual-use technologies, policies, and organizations for military benefit.

- In March 2016, President Xi underscored this message by emphasizing defense innovation during a visit with the PLA's delegation to the National People's Congress. He urged "great attention to the development of strategic, cutting-edge technologies" for the military, among other subjects.

China's 13th Five-Year Plan (2016-2020) includes the establishment of focus areas for research, development, and innovation. Several of these have defense implications: aerospace engines—including turbofan technology—and gas turbines; quantum communications and computing; innovative electronics and software; automation and robotics; special materials and applications; nanotechnology; neuroscience, neural research, and artificial intelligence; and deep-space exploration and on-orbit servicing and maintenance systems. Other areas where China is concentrating significant R&D resources include nuclear fusion, hypersonic technology, and the deployment and "hardening" of an expanding constellation of multipurpose satellites. China's drive to expand civil-military integration and international economic activity supports these goals.

The National Natural Science Foundation of China (NSFC), the China Academy of Sciences, and the Ministry of Science and Technology fund and promote basic and applied research, scientific innovation, and high-technology integration throughout China's scientific, engineering, and civil-military industrial complex. The China Academy of Sciences, working closely with the NSFC, is the highest academic institution for comprehensive R&D in the natural and applied sciences in China and reports directly to the State Council in an advisory capacity, with much of its work ultimately funding disciplines and contributing to products for military use.

Major Production-Sector Snapshots

Missile and Space. China's missile programs, including its ballistic and cruise missile systems, are comparable to those of other international top-tier producers. China's production of a wide range of ballistic, cruise, air-to-air, and surface-to-air missiles for the PLA and for export has probably been enhanced by upgrades to primary assembly and solid rocket motor production facilities. China has also purchased Russia's S-400 air defense system and received its first delivery in April 2018.[308] China's space launch vehicle industry is expanding to support commercial and rapid satellite launch services and the manned space program.

Naval/Shipbuilding. China is the top ship-producing nation in the world and has increased its shipbuilding capacity and capability for all types of naval projects, including submarines, surface combatants, naval aviation, sealift, and amphibious assets. China's two largest state-owned shipbuilders—the China State Shipbuilding Corporation and China Shipbuilding Industry Corporation— collaborate in shared ship designs and construction information to increase shipbuilding efficiency. China continues to invest in foreign suppliers for some propulsion units but is becoming increasingly self-sufficient.

Armaments. China's production capacity continues to advance in almost every area of PLAA systems, including new versions of main battle tanks and new light tanks, armored personnel carriers, assault vehicles, air defense artillery systems, and artillery pieces.[309] China is capable of producing ground weapon systems at or near world-class standards; however, quality deficiencies persist with some export equipment.

Aviation. China's aviation industry has advanced to produce a developmental large transport aircraft, modern fourth- to fifth-generation fighters incorporating low-observable technologies, modern reconnaissance and attack UAVs, and attack helicopters. China's commercial aircraft industry has invested in high-precision and technologically advanced machine tooling and production processes, avionics, and other components applicable to the production of military aircraft; however, China's aircraft industry remains reliant on foreign-sourced components for dependable, proven, high-performance aircraft engines. China's infrastructure and experience related to the production of commercial and military aircraft are improving because of the country's ongoing C919 commercial airliner and Y-20 large transport programs.

China's domestically produced WS-10 family of military turbofan engines, which power the J11-B, carrier-based J-15, and J-16 fighters.

APPENDIX I: *Arms Sales*

From 2012 to 2016, China's arms sales totaled about $20 billion, placing China among the world's top five global arms suppliers.[310] China primarily conducts arms sales in conjunction with economic aid and development assistance to support its broader foreign policy goals, such as securing access to natural resources and export markets, promoting its political influence among host country elites, and building support in international forums. To a lesser extent, arms sales also reflect the profit-seeking activities of individual arms trading companies in China and efforts to offset China's defense-related research and development costs.

From the perspective of China's arms customers, most of which are developing countries, Chinese arms are less expensive than those offered by other top international arms suppliers. They also are generally considered to be of lower quality and reliability, but many still have advanced capabilities. Chinese arms also come with fewer political strings attached compared with alternative sources, which is attractive to customers who may not have access to other sources of arms for political or economic reasons.

The bulk of China's sales from 2012 to 2016 were to countries in the Asia-Pacific region, primarily Pakistan. China's arms sales and defense-industrial cooperation with Pakistan include selling LY-80 SAMs, naval ships, main battle tanks, air-to-air missiles, and fighter aircraft.[311,312,313] In 2015, China signed an agreement with Pakistan for the sale of eight submarines. Under the terms of this multibillion-dollar contract, the first four will be built in China and the remaining four in Pakistan.[314,315]

China is a niche supplier of armed UAVs and has sold these systems to several countries in the Middle East, including Iraq, Saudi Arabia, Egypt, and the United Arab Emirates. China faces little competition for sale of such systems because most countries that produce them are restricted from selling the technology as signatories of the Missile Technology Control Regime and or the Wassenaar Arrangement on Export Controls for Conventional Arms and Dual-Use Goods and Technologies.[316]

China's Conventional Weapons and Missile-Related Customers, 2002–2017

317, 318, 319, 320, 321, 322, 323, 324, 325, 326, 327, 328

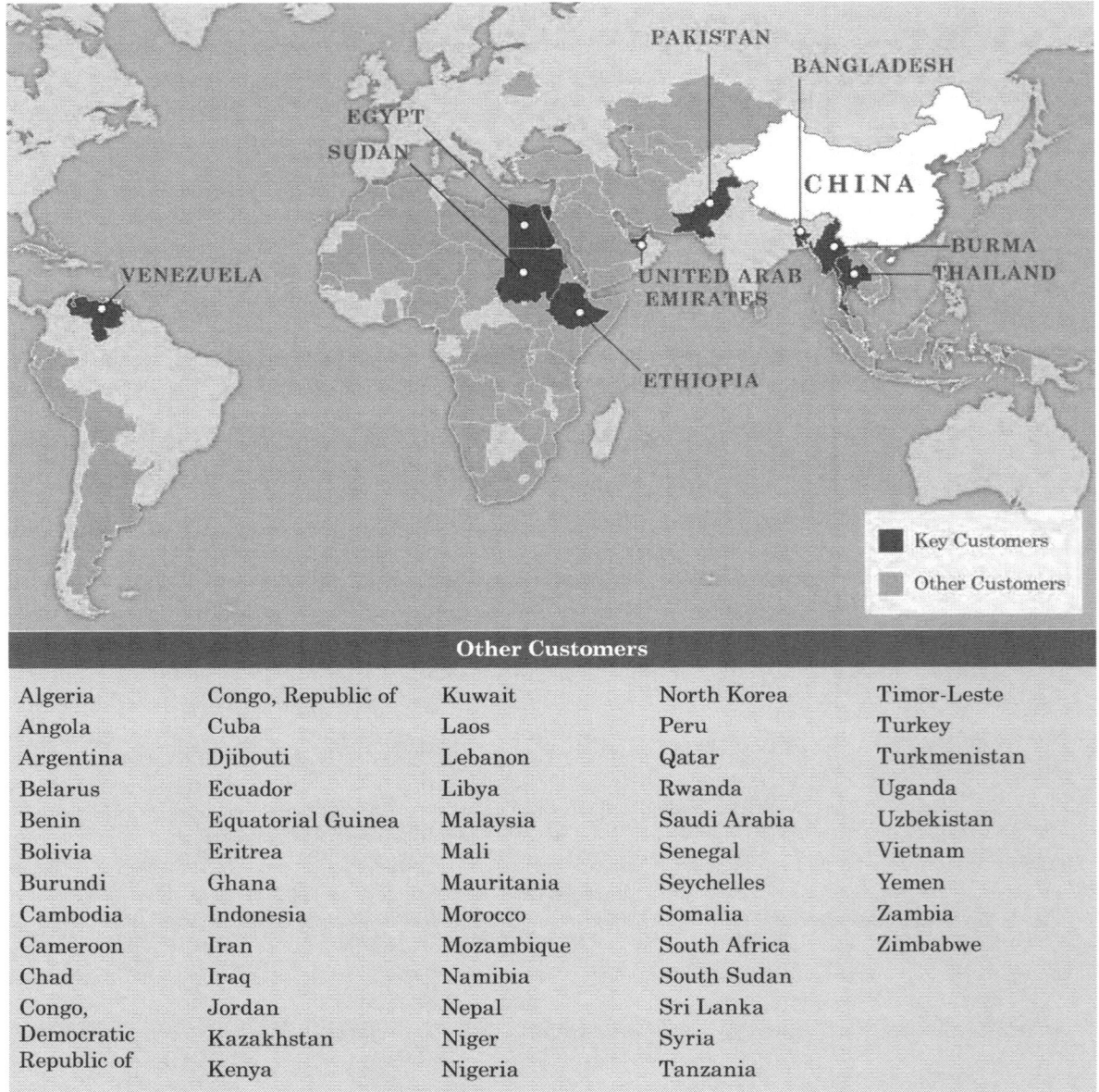

Other Customers				
Algeria	Congo, Republic of	Kuwait	North Korea	Timor-Leste
Angola	Cuba	Laos	Peru	Turkey
Argentina	Djibouti	Lebanon	Qatar	Turkmenistan
Belarus	Ecuador	Libya	Rwanda	Uganda
Benin	Equatorial Guinea	Malaysia	Saudi Arabia	Uzbekistan
Bolivia	Eritrea	Mali	Senegal	Vietnam
Burundi	Ghana	Mauritania	Seychelles	Yemen
Cambodia	Indonesia	Morocco	Somalia	Zambia
Cameroon	Iran	Mozambique	South Africa	Zimbabwe
Chad	Iraq	Namibia	South Sudan	
Congo,	Jordan	Nepal	Sri Lanka	
Democratic	Kazakhstan	Niger	Syria	
Republic of	Kenya	Nigeria	Tanzania	

Over 65 countries have been recipients of Chinese arms since 2002.

APPENDIX J: Glossary of Acronyms

2PLA	PLA Second Department
3PLA	PLA Third Department
4PLA	PLA Fourth Department
ACMI	air combat maneuvering instrumentation
AEW	airborne early warning
AEW&C	airborne early warning and control
AG	Australia Group
AIFV	armored infantry fighting vehicle
AIP	air-independent propulsion
APC	armored personnel carrier
ASBM	antiship ballistic missile
ASCM	antiship cruise missile
ASEAN	Association of Southeast Asian Nations
ASW	antisubmarine warfare
ASUW	antisurface warfare
BCW	Biological Weapons Convention
BRI	Belt and Road Initiative
CBW	chemical and biological warfare
CCG	China Coast Guard
CCP	Chinese Communist Party
CDIC	Central Discipline Inspection Commission
CMC	Central Military Commission
COMSAT	communications satellite

CWC	Chemical Weapons Convention
C2	command and control
C4ISR	command, control, communications, computers, intelligence, surveillance, and reconnaissance
DTL	Defense Transportation Law
ECM	electronic countermeasures
EDD	Equipment Development Department
EO	electro-optical
ESF	East Sea Fleet
EW	electronic warfare
FFG	guided-missile frigate
GDP	gross domestic product
GLCM	ground-launched cruise missile
GLD	General Logistics Department
GPS	Global Positioning System
GSD	General Staff Department
HADR	humanitarian assistance and disaster relief
HF	high frequency
ICBM	intercontinental ballistic missile
IO	information operations
IRBM	intermediate-range ballistic missile
ISR	intelligence, surveillance, and reconnaissance
JLSF	Joint Logistics Support Force

JOCC	Joint Operations Command Center	RDA	research, development, and acquisition
JSD	Joint Staff Department	RMA	revolution in military affairs
LACM	land-attack cruise missile	SAM	surface-to-air missile
LHA	landing helicopter assault	SAR	search and rescue
LSD	Logistics Support Department	SASTIND	State Administration for Science, Technology, Development, and Industry for National Defense
MARV	maneuverable reentry vehicle		
MIRV	multiple independently targetable reentry vehicle	SIGINT	signals intelligence
MOOTW	military operations other than war	SLBM	submarine-launched ballistic missile
MND	Ministry of National Defense	SLOC	sea line of communication
MPS	Ministry of Public Security	SLV	space launch vehicle
MRBM	medium-range ballistic missile	SOF	special operations forces
MSS	Ministry of State Security	SP	self-propelled
NFU	no first use	SRBM	short-range ballistic missile
NSF	North Sea Fleet	SSBN	nuclear-powered ballistic missile submarine
OPCW	Organization for the Prohibition of Chemical Weapons	SSGN	nuclear-powered guided-missile submarine
PAFMM	People's Armed Forces Maritime Militia	SSF	Strategic Support Force
PKO	peacekeeping operations	SSN	nuclear-powered attack submarine
PLA	People's Liberation Army	SSP	air-independent attack submarine
PLAA	PLA Army		
PLAAF	PLA Air Force	UAV	unmanned aerial vehicle
PLAN	PLA Navy	UGF	underground facility
PLANMC	PLA Navy Marine Corps	UHF	ultrahigh frequency
PLARF	PLA Rocket Force	UN	United Nations
PWD/LB	Political Work Department Liaison Bureau	VBSS	visit, board, search, and seizure
		VHF	very high frequency
R&D	research and development		

INTENTIONALLY LEFT BLANK

REFERENCES

1 "Full text of Xi Jinping's report at 19th CPC National Congress," Xinhua, November 03, 2017, URL: www.xinhuanet.com/english/special/2017-11/03/c_136725942.htm.

2 "China Focus: 'Be Ready to Win Wars'," Xinhua in English, August 01, 2017, URL: http://www.xinhuanet.com/english/2017-08/01/c_136491455.htm.

3 Annual Report to Congress; Military and Security Developments Involving the People's Republic of China 2016; Office of the Secretary of Defense; April 2016.

4 Annual Report to Congress; Military and Security Developments Involving the People's Republic of China 2017; Office of the Secretary of Defense; May 2017.

5 Joel Wuthnow and Phillip C. Saunders, "Chinese Military Reforms in the Age of Xi Jinping: Drivers, Challenges, and Implications; Institute for National Strategic Studies (INSS); China Strategic Perspectives; National Defense University; NDU Press; March 2017; p 10; accessed at https://books.google.com/books?id=QXhBxcaomJIC&pg=PA36&lpg=PA36&dq=China+and+the+Equipment+Development+DEpartment+EDD&source=bl&ots=rR7MjPCjt7&sig=2D4uWqsaMxL4teRPCilro10-0d6c&hl=nl&sa=X&ved=0ahUKEwilnO_S6oDaAhXJ_ywKHT-M7AzUQ6AEIQTAD#v=onepage&q=China%20and%20the%20Equipment%20Development%20DEpartment%20EDD&f=false.

6 "Full text of Xi Jinping's report at 19th CPC National Congress," Xinhua, November 03, 2017, URL: www.xinhuanet.com/english/special/2017-11/03/c_136725942.htm.

7 "China Needs Series of Laws on National Security: NPC Spokesperson," Xinhua, March 4, 2015, URL: english.gov.cn/news/top_news/2015/03/04/content_281475065544302.htm.

8 "Full text of Chinese state councilor's article on Xi Jinping's Diplomacy Thought," Xinhua, July 19, 2017, URL: http://www.xinhuanet.com/english/2017-07/19/c_136455986.htm.

9 "1,000 Chinese soldiers reportedly still in Doklam a month after border stand-off ended," South China Morning Post, October 06, 2017, URL: http://www.scmp.com/news/china/diplomacy-defence/article/2114265/1000-chinese-soldiers-reportedly-still-doklam-month.

10 "Full text of Xi Jinping's report at 19th CPC National Congress," Xinhua, November 03, 2017, URL: www.xinhuanet.com/english/special/2017-11/03/c_136725942.htm.

11 "Full text of Xi Jinping's report at 19th CPC National Congress," Xinhua, November 03, 2017, URL: www.xinhuanet.com/english/special/2017-11/03/c_136725942.htm.

12 Shannon Tiezzi, "China's National Security Strategy," The Diplomat, January 24, 2015, URL: https://thediplomat.com/2015/01/chinas-national-security-strategy/.

13 "China: Xi Jinping Chairs Political Bureau Meeting on Outline for National Security Strategy," Xinhua, January 24, 2015, URL: http://politics.people.com.cn/n/2015/0124/c1024-26441895.html.

14 "China Needs Series of Laws on National Security: NPC Spokesperson," Xinhua, March 4, 2015, URL: english.gov.cn/news/top_news/2015/03/04/content_281475065544302.htm.

15 "Full Text: Work Report of NPC Standing Committee," Xinhua, March 19, 2016, URL: www.xinhuanet.com/english/china/2016-03/19/c_135204257.htm.

16 "Full text of Chinese state councilor's article on Xi Jinping's Diplomacy Thought," Xinhua, July 19, 2017, URL: http://www.xinhuanet.com/english/2017-07/19/c_136455986.htm.

17 Annual Report to Congress; Military and Security Developments Involving the People's Republic of China 2017; Office of the Secretary of Defense; May 2017.

18 Annual Report to Congress: Military and Security Developments Involving the People's Republic of China 2018, Office of the Secretary of Defense; 2018.

19 Annual Report to Congress; Military and Security Developments Involving the People's Republic of China 2016; Office of the Secretary of Defense; April 2016.

20 Annual Report to Congress; Military and Security Developments Involving the People's Republic of China 2017; Office of the Secretary of Defense; May 2017.

[21] "Xi Jinping rolls out leaner top line-up for China's military machine," South China Morning Post, October 26, 2017, URL: http://www.scmp.com/news/china/diplomacy-defence/article/2117004/xi-jinping-rolls-out-leaner-top-line-chinas-military.

[22] Annual Report to Congress; Military and Security Developements Involving the People's Republic of China 2017; Office of the Secretary of Defense; May 2017

[23] Annual Report to Congress; Military and Security Developements Involving the People's Republic of China 2018, Office of the Secretary of Defense, 2018

[24] "Xi Jinping rolls out leaner top line-up for China's military machine," South China Morning Post, October 26, 2017, URL: http://www.scmp.com/news/china/diplomacy-defence/article/2117004/xi-jinping-rolls-out-leaner-top-line-chinas-military.

[25] Annual Report to Congress: Military and Security Developments Involving the People's Republic of China 2016, Office of the Secretary of Defense, April 2016.

[26] "Full text of Xi Jinping's report at 19th CPC National Congress," Xinhua, November 03, 2017, URL: www.xinhuanet.com/english/special/2017-11/03/c_136725942.htm.

[27] Maya Wang, "China's Dystopian Push to Revolutionize Surveillance," Washington Post, 18 August 2017, URL: https://www.washingtonpost.com/news/democracy-post/wp/2017/08/18/chinas-dystopian-push-to-revolutionize-surveillance/?utm_term=.aa85891a8c59.

[28] China's Military Strategy White Paper; The State Council Information Office of the People's Republic of China; May 2015, Beijing; http://news.xinhuanet.com/english/china/2015-05/26/c_134271001.htm.

[29] Viola Zhou, "Why China's Armed Police Will Now Only Take Orders From Xi And His Generals," South China Morning Post, 28 December 2017, URL: http://www.scmp.com/news/china/policies-politics/article/2126039/reason-why-chinas-armed-police-will-now-only-take.

[30] Liu Zhen, "China's military police given control of coastguard as Beijing boosts maritime security," South China Morning Post, 21 March 2018, URL: http://www.scmp.com/news/china/diplomacy-defence/article/2138257/chinas-military-police-given-control-coastguard-beijing.

[31] Timothy R. Heath, "China's Pursuit of Overseas Security," RAND, 2018; p 22; accessed at https://www.rand.org/content/dam/rand/pubs/research_reports/.../RAND_RR2271.pdf.

[32] Annual Report to Congress: Military and Security Developments Involving the People's Republic of China 2017, Office of the Secretary of Defense, 2017.

[33] Annual Report to Congress; Military and Security Developments Involving the People's Republic of China 2016; Office of the Secretary of Defense; April 2016.

[34] Annual Report to Congress; Military and Security Developments Involving the People's Republic of China 2016; Office of the Secretary of Defense; April 2016.

[35] Annual Report to Congress; Military and Security Developments Involving the People's Republic of China 2016; Office of the Secretary of Defense; April 2016.

[36] "The Dragon's New Teeth," The Economist, Bejing, April 7th, 2012, URL: https://www.economist.com/node/21552193..

[37] Annual Report to Congress: Military and Security Developments Involving the People's Republic of China 2018, Office of the Secretary of Defense, 2018.

[38] Annual Report to Congress: Military and Security Developments Involving the People's Republic of China 2018, Office of the Secretary of Defense, 2018.

[39] Annual Report to Congress; Military and Security Developments Involving the People's Republic of China 2017; Office of the Secretary of Defense; May 2017.

[40] Annual Report to Congress: Military and Security Developments Involving the People's Republic of China 2018, Office of the Secretary of Defense; 2018.

[41] Annual Report to Congress: Military and Security Developments Involving the People's Republic of China 2017, Office of the Secretary of Defense; May 2017.

[42] Annual Report to Congress; Military and Security Developments Involving the People's Republic of China 2017; Office of the Secretary of Defense; May 2017.

[43] Joint Force Quarterly "China's Goldwater-Nichols? Assessing PLA's Organizational Reforms" by Phillip Saunders and Joel Wuthnow; Jul 1, 2016.

[44] People's Daily "Xi Jinping: Build a Modern Military Power System with Chinese Characteristics"; Aug 31, 2014; http://news.xinhuanet.com/politics/2014-08/31/c_1112295195_3.htm.

[45] Annual Report to Congress; Military and Security Developments Involving the People's Republic of China 2017; Office of the Secretary of Defense; May 2017.

46 China's Military Strategy White Paper; The State Council Information Office of the People's Republic of China; May 2015, Beijing; http://news.xinhuanet.com/english/china/2015-05/26/c_134271001.htm.

47 Annual Report to Congress; Military and Security Developments Involving the People's Republic of China 2016; Office of the Secretary of Defense; April 2016.

48 Annual Report to Congress; Military and Security Developments Involving the People's Republic of China 2017; Office of the Secretary of Defense; May 2017.

49 Xinhua "Starting with a New Style Under Fluttering Red Combat Banners – Observing the New Theater Commands"; Feb 2, 2016; URL: http://news.xinhuanet.com/politics/2016-02/02/c_1117973365.htm.

50 China Military Online "Ministry of National Defense hold Press Conference on CMC Organ" by Yao Jianing; Jan 12, 2016; http://english.chinamil.com.cn/news-channels/china-military-news/2016-01/12/content_6854444.htm.

51 Joint Force Quarterly "China's Goldwater-Nichols? Assessing PLA's Organizational Reforms" by Phillip Saunders and Joel Wuthnow; Jul 1, 2016.

52 Annual Report to Congress; Military and Security Developments Involving the People's Republic of China 2017; Office of the Secretary of Defense; May 2017.

53 Annual Report to Congress; Military and Security Developments Involving the People's Republic of China 2017; Office of the Secretary of Defense; May 2017.

54 Joint Force Quarterly "China's Goldwater-Nichols? Assessing PLA's Organizational Reforms" by Phillip Saunders and Joel Wuthnow; Jul 1, 2016.

55 Annual Report to Congress; Military and Security Developments Involving the People's Republic of China 2017; Office of the Secretary of Defense; May 2017.

56 Annual Report to Congress; Military and Security Developments Involving the People's Republic of China 2016; Office of the Secretary of Defense; April 2016.

57 "Photos: Chinese Military Forces Hold Ceremony After Arriving at Djibouti Support Base." Tianjin Jinri Toutiao (Chinese language), August 1, 2017, URL: www.toutiao.com.

58 "Photos: Chinese Navy Holds Ceremony Establishing Djibouti Support Base." Tianjin Jinri Toutiao (Chinese language), July 13, 2017, URL: www.toutiao.com.

59 "Photos: Chinese PLA Navy Ceremony for Troops Departing to Djibouti Support Base." Beijing China Military Online (Chines language), July 11, 2017. URL: http://www.81.cn.

60 PLA Southern Theater Command Air Force Enhances Maritime Combat Capabilities; 21 OCT 2016; http://eng.chinamil.com.cn/view/2016-09/05/content_7242128.htm.

61 In Depth; Why the U.S. is Frequently Provocative in South China Sea – China's Bombers Break the Islands Chains 8 Times with Countermeasures; 02 DEC 15; http://mil.news.Sina.com.cn/2015-12-02/1111845474.htm.

62 China Military Online: Three Solutions for China's New-Generation Long-range Strategic Bomber; 05 SEP 2016; http://www.chinadaily.com.cn/china/2016-10/21/content_27130415_7.htm.

63 "China and Ukraine agree deal to restart production of An-225," Jane's; September 07, 2016, URL: http://www.janes.com/article/63341/china-and-ukraine-agree-to-restart-an-225.

64 Indian TV Website Report Shows Images of China's First Home-Grown Aircraft Carrier and new J-15A Fighter Jet; 12 OCT 2016; http://www.ndtv.com/world-news/china-racing-ahead-of-india-in-aircraft-carrier-development-1472835.

65 Global Times: Flashpoints in Asian Waters; 27 OCT 2016; Global Times hosted the Japan Times article at: http://www.globaltimes.cn/content/1013393.shtml.

66 Andrew Tate, "China's second aircraft carrier begins sea trials," HIS Jane's Defence Weekly; May 14, 2018, URL: http://janes.com/article/80064/china-s-second-aircraft-carrier-begins-sea-trials.

67 China's Troop Contributions to U.N. Peacekeeping; Oct 2016; https://www.usip.org/publications/2016/07/chinas-troop-contributions-un-peacekeeping.

68 People's Daily Online: "Belt and Road" Initiative Points to Brighter Globalization; 26 OCT 2016; http://www.globaltimes.cn/content/1013888.shtml.

69 Global Times Online: Ethiopia Djibouti Railway Signals New Era Of Chinese Aid In Infrastructure Construction; 27 OCT 2016; http://eng.mod.gov.cn/TopNews/2016-10/09/content_4743532.htm.

70 China Military Online: 'Djibouti Base Not for Military Power: PLA Daily'; 27 OCT 2016; http://news.xinhuanet.com/english/2016-10/25/c_135780276.htm.

71 Annual Report to Congress; Military and Security Developments Involving the People's Republic of China 2016; Office of the Secretary of Defense; April 2016.

72 Xiao Tianliang, Chief Editor, The Science of Strategy, Beijing: NDU Press, April 2015, pp. 121.

73 "Senior Leader Perspective: China's Perspective on Nuclear Deterrence,"Air & Space Power Journal, Spring 2010, pp 27-30.

74 "Position Paper of the People's Republic of China for the 72nd Session of the United Nations General Assembly," Permanent Mission of the People's Republic of China to the United Nations and Other International Organizations in Vienna, September 09, 2017, URL: http://www.chinesemission-vienna.at/eng/zgbd/t1490124.htm.

75 China's Military Strategy White Paper; The State Council Information Office of the People's Republic of China; May 2015, Beijing; http://news.xinhuanet.com/english/china/2015-05/26/c_134271001.htm.

76 "Position Paper of the People's Republic of China for the 72nd Session of the United Nations General Assembly," Permanent Mission of the People's Republic of China to the United Nations and Other International Organizations in Vienna, September 09, 2017, URL: http://www.chinesemission-vienna.at/eng/zgbd/t1490124.htm.

77 Yu Jixun, ed., "The Science of Second Artillery Campaigns," Beijing: PLA Press, 2004, p. 238.

78 Xiao Tianliang, Chief Editor, The Science of Strategy, Beijing: NDU Press, April 2015, pp. 364, 369.

79 "From tanks to carrier killers: 10 weapons unveiled at China's military parade," South China Morning Post, September 03, 2015, URL: http://www.scmp.com/news/china/diplomacy-defence/article/1854800/10-most-anticipated-weapons-military-parade.

80 "Chinese nuclear forces, 2013," Bulletin of Atomic Scientists; 1 November 2013.

81 "China confirms new generation nuclear-capable ICBM that can target US," Sydney Morning Herald, August 01, 2014, URL: https://www.smh.com.au/world/china-confirms-new-generation-nuclearcapable-icbm-that-can-target-us-20140801-zzj93.html.

82 Ralph Cossa, Brad Glosserman, and David Santoro, "Conference report of the 11th China-US Strategic Nuclear Dynamics Dialogue," Center for Strategic and International Studies, September, 2017, URL: https://www.csis.org/analysis/issues-insights-vol-18-cr1-realistic-way-forward-us-china-strategic-nuclear-relationship.

83 Xinhua; Dec 07, 2016; "Rear Admiral: China's Development of H-20 Bomber Just in Time;" http://english.chinamil.com.cn/view/2016-12/07/content_7396601.htm.

84 Science of Strategy, Academy of Military Sciences, Beijing: Military Science Press, 2013, pp. 175.

85 Xiao Tianliang, Chief Editor; The Science of Strategy, PLA National Defense University publication; Beijing: NDU Press, April 2015, pp. 364, 369.

86 "China hails first test of hypersonic nuclear missile carrier," South China Morning Post, January 15, 2014, URL: http://www.scmp.com/news/china/article/1405784/china-hails-first-test-hypersonic-nuclear-missile-carrier.

87 "Hypersonic missiles Can Defeat US Missile Defenses," Cankao Xiaoxi, February 23, 2014, URL: http://ihl.cankaoxiaoxi.com/2014/0207/343864.shtml.

88 China Academy of Engineering Physics; 10JUN2015; 2015 Chinese Academy of Engineering Physics Postdoctoral Careers; www.caep.ac.cn/rlzy/bsh/21443.shtml.

89 SinoDefense; Dong Feng-4 (CSS-3); www.sinodefense.com/rocketry/df4.

90 NTI; 29 September 2011; Ninth Academy; Science City; Zitong Facility; Mianyang Facility; "The Los Alamos of China"; http://www.nti.org/learn/facilities/702/.

91 NTI; 29 September 2011; Ninth Academy; Science City; Zitong Facility; Mianyang Facility; "The Los Alamos of China"; http://www.nti.org/learn/facilities/702/.

92 China Academy of Engineering Physics; 10JUN2015; 2015 Chinese Academy of Engineering Physics Postdoctoral Careers; www.caep.ac.cn/rlzy/bsh/21443.shtml.

93 Science & Global Security; ISSN: 0892-9882; 23OCT15; China's Uranium Enrichment Complex.

94 Bulletin of the Atomic Scientists; 07DEC15; China's rapidly expanding centrifuge enrichment capacity;, http://thebulletin.org/china%E2%80%99s-rapidly-expanding-centrifuge-enrichment-capacity8934.

95 Harvard University; China's Stockpile of Military Plutonium: A New Estimate; July 2011; http://www.belfercenter.org/publication/chinas-stockpile-military-plutonium-new-estimate.

96 Telegraph; 4 January 2011; China Masters Nuclear Fuel Reprocessing Technology; http://www.telegraph.co.uk/news/worldnews/asia/china/8238032/china-masters-nuclear-fuel-reprocessing-technology.html.

97 NTI; Aug 2013; China Biological Chronology; http://www.nti.org/country-profiles/china/biological.

98 NTI; Aug 2013; China Biological Profile; http://www.nti.org/country-profiles/china.

99 NTI; OCT 2014; China Overview; http://www.nti.org/china.

100 US Department of State; Adherence to and Compliance with Arms Control, Nonproliferation and Disarmament Agreements and Commitments; August 2005; https://www.state.gov/documents/organization/52113.pdf.

101 US Department of State; Adherence to and Compliance with Arms Control, Nonproliferation and Disarmament Agreements and Commitments; August 2005; https://www.state.gov/documents/organization/52113.pdf.

102 NTI; OCT 2014; China Overview; http://www.nti.org/china.

103 Shirley A. Kan; 03 January 2014; China and Proliferation of Weapons of Mass Destruction and Missiles: Policy Issues; Congressional Research Service (CRS) - Report # RL31555.

104 NTI; JUN 2013; China Country Profiles; China; http://www.nti.org/country-profiles/china.

105 NTI; OCT 2014; China Overview; http://www.nti.org/china.

106 NTI; Aug 2013; China Biological Chronology; http://www.nti.org/country-profiles/china/biological.

107 Janes; 30 Oct 2014; China Production Capability.

108 NTI; OCT 2014; China Overview; http://www.nti.org/china.

109 Janes; 30 Oct 2014; China Production Capability.

110 Shirley A. Kan; 03 January 2014; China and Proliferation of Weapons of Mass Destruction and Missiles: Policy Issues; Congressional Research Service (CRS) - Report # RL31555.

111 Information Office, State Council of the People's Republic of China, "China's National Defense in 2010," Editor Wang Guanqun, March 2011, www.xinhuanet.com; China Arms Control and Disarmament Association, "Chinese Nonproliferation Policy and Export Control Policy," Li Hong, Vice President and Secretary General, 28 August 2013, http://csis.org; Foreign and Commonwealth Office, "'Bridging the Gap: Analysis of China's export controls against international standards," Chin-Hao Huang, 25 May 2012, www.gov.uk.

112 NTI; OCT 2014; China Overview; http://www.nti.org/china.

113 Organization for the Prohibition of Chemical Weapons, "Workshop on Assistance and Protection against Chemical Weapons held in China," accessed online on 13 Feb 18, URL: https://www.opcw.org/news/browse/116/article/regional-workshop-on-assistance-and-protection-against-chemical-weapons-held-in-china/Regional.

114 NTI; OCT 2014; China Overview; http://www.nti.org/china.

115 NTI; OCT 2014; China Overview; http://www.nti.org/china.

116 NTI; OCT 2014; China Overview; http://www.nti.org/china.

117 NTI; OCT 2014; China Overview; http://www.nti.org/china.

118 Shirley A. Kan; Congressional Research Service (CRS) - Report # RL31555; 03 January 2014; China and Proliferation of Weapons of Mass Destruction and Missiles: Policy Issues.

119 Annual Report to Congress: Military and Security Developments Involving the People's Republic of China 2017, Office of the Secretary of Defense; May 2017.

120 Annual Report to Congress: Military and Security Developments Involving the People's Republic of China 2017, Office of the Secretary of Defense; May 2017.

121 Annual Report to Congress: Military and Security Developments Involving the People's Republic of China 2017, Office of the Secretary of Defense; May 2017.

122 Harvey, Brian, China in Space: The Great Leap Forward; 2013; Springer Science + Business Media; New York.

123 Report; Stokes, Mark A. and Dean Cheng; Project 2049 Institute for the U.S.-China Economic and Security Review Commission; China's Evolving Space Capabilities: Implications for U.S. Interests; 26 April 2012; http://project2049.net/documents/uscc_china-space-program-report_april-2012.pdf.

124 Report; Stokes, Mark A. and Dean Cheng; Project 2049 Institute for the U.S.-China Economic and Security Review Commission; China's Evolving Space Capabilities: Implications for U.S. Interests; 26 April 2012;; http://project2049.net/documents/uscc_china-space-program-report_april-2012.pdf.

125 White Paper; The State Council Information Office of the People's Republic of China; China's BeiDou Navigation Satellite System; June 2016; http://www.scio.gov.cn/zxbd/wz/Document/1480433/1480433.htm.

126 White Paper; The State Council Information Office of the People's Republic of China; China's BeiDou Navigation Satellite System; June 2016; http://www.scio.gov.cn/zxbd/wz/Document/1480433/1480433.htm.

127 Internet; Xinhua; China To Launch 30 Beidou Navigation Satellites In Next 5 Years; 19 May 2016; http://english.cas.cn/newsroom/china_research/201605/t20160523_163363.shtml.

128 Report; Stokes, Mark A. and Dean Cheng; Project 2049 Institute for the U.S.-China Economic and Security Review Commission; China's Evolving Space Capabilities: Implications for U.S. Interests; 26 April 2012; http://project2049.net/documents/uscc_china-space-program-report_april-2012.pdf.

129 World Meteorological Organization; Satellite Status; accessed 17 October 2016; www.wmo.ing/pages/prog/sat/satellitestatus.php.

130 Annual Report to Congress; Military and Security Developments Involving the People's Republic of China 2017; Office of the Secretary of Defense; May 2017.

131 Peng Guangqian, Yao Youzhi, eds; 2001; Science of Strategy.

132 Li Bingyan, 27 Jan 2016; Beijing Guangming Ribao: General Trend of the Worldwide Revolution in Military Affairs and the Form of Future War.

133 China Manned Space Engineering Office Website; Space Station Project Development Progress; 23 April 2016; http://www.cmse.gov.cn/uploadfile/news/uploadfile/201604/20160427104809225.pdf.

134 Internet; Xinhua; Chang-E 5 To Launch Sometime in 2017 -- China's Latest Secret Lunar Exploration Project Uncovered; 1 March 2014; http://news.xinhuanet.com/tech/2014-03/01/c_119562037.htm.

135 Xinhua: China To Land On Dark Side Of Moon In 2018; 14 January 2016; http://news.xinhuanet.com/english/2016-01/15/c_135010577.htm.

136 Internet, NASASpaceFlight, Chang'e-5 Lunar Sample Return, CZ-5 - Wenchang - NET 2017, http://forum.nasaspaceflight.com/index.php?action=dlattach;topic=33431.0;attach=1440126, Accessed 28 July 2017.

137 Report; Stokes, Mark A. and Dean Cheng; Project 2049 Institute for the U.S.-China Economic and Security Review Commission; China's Evolving Space Capabilities: Implications for U.S. Interests; 26 April 2012; http://project2049.net/documents/uscc_china-space-program-report_april-2012.pdf.

138 Briefing; Zhou, Yuanying; China Great Wall Industry Corporation; China's Space Industry: Achievement, Future Planning and International Cooperation; presented by Zhou Yuanying for China Great Wall Industry Corporation at the 4th International Space Conference, Vilnius, Lithuania 18 Sept. 2012; updated 27 Sept. 2013.

139 China Space Flight; Chinese Rocket service time; 12 March 2016; http://www.chinaspaceflight.com/rocket/China-launchers-timeline.html.

140 Kevin Pollpeter and Kenneth Allen ed; 26 AUG 2015; DGI; The PLA as Organization: Reference Volume v2.0; pp 401.; http://www.andrewerickson.com/2015/12/a-classic-reference-with-renewed-relevance-download-the-pla-as-organization-v2-0/.

141 Joe McReynolds; 17 APR 2016; Jamestown Foundation China Brief; China's Evolving Perspectives on Network Warfare: Lessons from the Science of Military Strategy; pp 6; https://jamestown.org/program/chinas-evolving-perspectives-on-network-warfare-lessons-from-the-science-of-military-strategy/.

142 Lincoln Davidson; 'China's Strategic Support Force: The New Home of the PLA's Cyber Operations?'; CFR.org; Net Politics; January 20, 2016; http://blogs.cfr.org/cyber/2016/01/20/chinas-strategic-support-force-the-new-home-of-the-plas-cyber-operations/.

143 John Costello; 'The Strategic Support Force: China's Information Warfare Service'; The Jamestown Foundation; China Brief Vol. 16 Issue 3; February 8, 2016; https://jamestown.org/program/the-strategic-support-force-chinas-information-warfare-service/.

144 John Costello; 'China Finally Centralizes Its Space, Cyber, Information Forces'; TheDiplomat.com; January 20, 2016.

145 Peng Guangqian, Yao Youzhi, eds; 2001; Science of Strategy; pp 311.

146 Department of Justice, "U.S. Charges Five Chinese Military Hackers for Cyber Espionage Against U.S. Corporations and a Labor Organization for Commercial Advantage;" May 19, 2014; URL: http://www.justice.gov/opa/pr/2014/May/14-ag-528.html .

147 Lesley Wroughton, Michael Martina, "Cyber spying, maritime disputes loom large in U.S.-China talks," Reuters, July 8, 2014, URL: https://www.reuters.com/article/china-usa/cyber-spying-maritime-disputes-loom-large-in-u-s-china-talks-idUSL4N0PJ0MT20140708.

148 Zhang Yuliang (ed.), Science of Campaigns (National Defense University, Beijing, 2006; ISBN 7-5626-1407-0) p. 155-66.

149 Zhang Yuliang (ed.), Science of Campaigns (National Defense University, Beijing, 2006; ISBN 7-5626-1407-0) p. 155-66.

150 Zhang Xingye and Zhang Zhanli ed., Campaign Stratagems, (PLA National Defense University, Beijing, 2002), p. 1-2, 26-8.

151 Zhang Yuliang (ed.), Science of Campaigns (National Defense University, Beijing, 2006; ISBN 7-5626-1407-0) p. 96-7.

152 "Theories of the Initial Period of War" in Tiao Youzhi, ed., Theories of War and Strategy, PLA Press, Beijing, 2005 p. 564.

153 Wang Haibo, Gao Zhiwen, and Hua Xiao, Jiefangjun Bao Online, "The Grand Program for Building Modern Logistics -- an Interview of Zhou Songhe, Chief of Staff of the General Logistics Department's Headquarters Department on Issues Concerning the Logistic Work in the New Year," accessed at http://news.mod.gov.cn/headlines/2014-02/12/content_4489582.htm.

154 Zhang Liansong and Zhou Jing, "An Analysis of the Basic Contents of Hu Jintao's Important Theses on Military Logistics Construction," China Military Science, No. 5, 2007.

155 Liao Xilong, "Personally Experiencing Jinan Theater's Major Joint Logistics Reform," PLA Daily, December 16, 2008, accessed at http://military.people.com.cn/GB/1076/52984/8527794.html.

156 Duan Chengliang and Zhou Rui, "Division of the 13th Group Army Improves Support Effectiveness Through Precision Delivery, Realizes Precision Support With the Flexible Grouping of Modules," Jiefangjun Bao, November 15, 2016.

157 Wang Jixin and Sun Xingwei, "Practicing Logistical Operations by Closely Adhering to Actual Combat Operations, Developing Crack Troops by Aiming at Battlefield: Zhengzhou Joint Logistical Support Center Focuses on Improving Rapid, Precise Logistical Support Capability," Jiefangjun Bao, January 26, 2018.

158 Wang Haibo, Gao Zhiwen, and Hua Xiao, Jiefangjun Bao Online, "The Grand Program for Building Modern Logistics -- an Interview of Zhou Songhe, Chief of Staff of the General Logistics Department's Headquarters Department on Issues Concerning the Logistic Work in the New Year," accessed at http://news.mod.gov.cn/headlines/2014-02/12/content_4489582.htm.

159 Yang Yang, "Logistics Commanding Officers of Tomorrow's Battlefields -- No Longer the 'Provision Officers' of That Month and That Date," Jiefangjun Bao, September 29, 2010. http://www.chinamil.com.cn/.

160 Liao Xilong, "Comprehensively Develop Modern Logistics With Scientific Development Concept as Guide," Quishi, July 16, 2006, accessed at http://www.qstheory.cn/zxdk/2006/200614/200907/t20090708_8817.htm.

161 "(Lushan Quake) 2nd LD-Writethru: 192 dead, 23 missing in China quake," Xinhua, Beijing Xinhua in English, April 22, 2013, URL: https://trove.nla.gov.au/work/178999486?q&versionId=194850676.

162 "Air Force uses civil UAVs in joint logistics support drill," PLA Daily in English, January 29, 2018; URL: eng.chinamil.com.cn/view/2018-01/29/content_7924990.htm.

163 Annual Report to Congress; Military and Security Developments Involving the People's Republic of China 2016; Office of the Secretary of Defense; April 2016.

164 Dennis J. Blasko, "Clarity of Intentions: People's Liberation Army Transregional Exercises to Defend China's Borders," in the Strategic Studies Institute publication "Learning by Doing: The PLA Trains at Home and Abroad," ed. Roy Kamphausen, David Lai, Travis Tanner, November 2012.

165 Greg Hallahan, "Collusion, Creative Bribery, & Subcontracting," FTI Consulting, October 30, 2014. URL: http://www.fticonsulting-asia.com/~/media/Files/us-files/insights/articles/collusion-creative-bribery-subcontracting.pdf.

166 Franz-Stefan Gady, "China Wants to Reform its Defense Industry"; The Diplomat; Asia Defense; accessed 22 Mar 2018; 10 June 2015; https://the dipl,omat.com/2015/06/china-wants-to-reform-its-defense-industry/.

167 Joel Wuthnow and Phillip C. Saunders, "Chinese Military Reforms in the Age of Xi Jinping: Drivers, Challenges, and Implications; Institute for National Strategic Studies (INSS); China Strategic Perspectives; National Defense University; NDU Press; March 2017; p 36; accessed at https://books.google.com/books?id=QXhBxcaomJIC&pg=PA36&lpg=PA36&dq=China+and+the+Equipment+Development+DEpartment+EDD&source=bl&ots=rR7MjPCjt7&sig=2D4uWqsaMxL4teRPCilro10-0d6c&hl=nl&sa=X&ved=0ahUKEwiInO_S6oDaAhXJ_ywKHTM7AzUQ6AEIQTAD#v=onepage&q=China%20and%20the%20Equipment%20Development%20DEpartment%20EDD&f=false.

168 Yun Zhao, "National Space Law in China"; Brill Nijhoff; Leiden Boston; 2015; p 29; accessed at https://books.google.com/books?id=jgVzBgAAQBAJ&pg=PA29&dq=SASTIND&hl=nl&sa=X&ved=0ahUKEwjwpPqP74DaAhUJ8ywKHZrjArkQ6AEINDAC#v=onepage&q=SASTIND&f=false.

169 "Xu Qiliang Stresses Quality and Innovation at Military Equipment Quality Work Meeting," Xinhua, May 19, 2015, URL: http://politics.people.com.cn/n/2015/0515/c1024-27008636.html.

170 Greg Levesque and Mark Stokes, "Blurred Lines: Military-Civil Fusion and the "Going Out of China's Defense Industry, Pointe Bello, December 2016; accessed at https://static1.squarespace.com/static/569925bfe0327c837e2e9a94/t/593dad0320099e64e1ca92a5/1497214574912/062017_Pointe+Bello_Military+Civil+Fusion+Report.pdf.

171 MIT News, Peter Dizikes; "Industrial "Edge Cities" Have Helped China Grow"; 17 August, 2017; accessed at http://news.nit.edu/2017/industrial-edge-cities-helped-china-grow-0818.

172 Yuecheng Yang; International Association of Science Parks and Areas of Innovation (IASP); Paper for the 30th IASP World Conference on Science & Technology Parks, 2013; "High-tech Zones (Science & Technology Parks) and China's Urbanization; accessed at http://inhalt.com.br/portodigital/Workshop2SpeakerYuecheng(Yang)CHI.pdf.

173 "Thirteenth Five-Year (2016-2020) Plan for National Economic and Social Development People's Republic of China," Chinese language translated; Tone Box excerpts addressing major science and technology projects for 2030; March 2016, pp. 14, 40, 42, 46, 49, and 58; Accessed 28 July 2016, URL: http://paper.people.com.cn/rmrb/html/2016-03/18/nw.D110000renmrb_20160318_1-01.htm.

174 Annual Report to Congress: Military and Security Developments Involving the People's Republic of China 2017, Office of the Secretary of Defense; May 2017.

175 "China's First Peacekeeping Helicopter Unit Arrives in Darfur," Beijing Xinhua (New China News Agency) (English language). August 6, 2017. URL: http://news.xinhuanet.com/english/2017-08/06/c_136503341.htm.

176 Annual Report to Congress: Military and Security Developments Involving the People's Republic of China 2017, Office of the Secretary of Defense; May 2017.

177 Annual Report to Congress: Military and Security Developments Involving the People's Republic of China 2017, Office of the Secretary of Defense; May 2017.

178 Dennis Blasko, "PLA Army 'Below the Neck' Reforms: Improving China's Deterrence and Joint Warfighting Posture; 2017; pp.1-21.

179 English translation of PLA manual "Science of Army Operations"; May 2011.

180 Annual Report to Congress; Military and Security Developments Involving the People's Republic of China 2016; Office of the Secretary of Defense; April 2016.

181 Dennis J Blasko; The Chinese Army Today: Tradition and Transformation for the 21st Century; ISBN: 13:978-0-415-78322-4.

182 Franz-Stefan Gady, "China Now Has the World's Largest Active Service Tank Force"; The Diplomat; Asia Defense; accessed 26 July 2018; 15 February 2018; https://the dipl,omat.com/2018/02/china-now-has-the-worlds-largest-active-service-tank-force/.

183 Study on Joint Firepower Warfare Theory, Hu Limin, Ying Fucheng, Beijing: National Defense University Press, 2004.

184 PLA Publication; Science of Army Operations; June 2009.

185 PLA Publication; Science of Army Operations; p. 184, 185; June 2009.

186 PLA Press publication; Air Defense Strategy and Study; November 1999.

187 PLA Publication; Science of Army Operations; p. 142, 178-180; June 2009.

188 PLA Publication; Science of Army Operations; p. 95; June 2009.

189 Mastro, O.S., 2015, A Global Expeditionary People's Liberation Army: 2025-2030, In R. Kamphausen and D. Lai (Eds) The Chinese People's Liberationa Army in 2025, (pp. 207-234), Carlisle, PA: U.S. Army War College Press.

190 Beijing Jiefangjun Bao Online; 15 May 2015 Online Edtion of Jiefangjun Bao; Subject: Army Aviation Official Discusses Military Modernization; http://www.chinamil.com.cn/.

191 PLA Publication; Science of Army Operations; p. 143; June 2009.

192 "Chinese Military Modernization and Force Development: Chinese and Outside Perspectives," Center for Strategic and International Studies, July 2014, p.205.

193 Annual Report to Congress; Military and Security Developments Involving the People's Republic of China 2016; Office of the Secretary of Defense; April 2016.

194 Center for Strategy and International Studies; July 2014; p. 212-216; Chinese Military Modernization and Force Development: Chinese and Outside Perspectives.

195 Defense Ministry's regular press conference on Jan. 29, 2015; http://english.chinamil.com.cn/news-channels/china-military-news/2015-01/29/content_6332211.htm.

196 Dennis Blasko; The Chinese Army Today: Tradition and Transformation for the 21st Century , Who is the PLA?, Volume 1, Edition 2; p. 182; January 2012; ISBN 13: 978-0-415-78322-4.

197 The "People" in the PLA: Recruitment, Training, and Education in China's Military; p. 124-125; September 2008.

198 China's Military Strategy White Paper; The State Council Information Office of the People's Republic of China; May 2015, Beijing; http://news.xinhuanet.com/english/china/2015-05/26/c_134271001.htm.

199 China Daily: China Changes Military Recruitment Period; http://www.chinadaily.com.cn/china/2013-06/15/content_16624114.htm.

200 Dennis Blasko; The Chinese Army Today: Tradition and Transformation for the 21st Century, Who is the PLA?, Volume1, Edition 2; p. 59-60; January 2001; ISBN 13: 978-0-415-78322-4.

201 "China – Navy," Jane's; Jane's World Navies; May 22, 2017. URL: https://janes.intelink.ic.gov/docs/binder/jwna/jwna20/jwna0034.htm.

202 "Overview of All China's White Papers on National Defense," China Ministry of National Defense, May 27, 2015. URL: http://eng.mod.gov.cn/TopNews/2015-05/27/content_4587121.htm.

203 "PLA Navy Party Standing Committee Holds Special Meeting to Deliberate Upon Issues of Military Operations, Military Training, and Force Management," Beijing Renmin Haijun - Report by staff reporters Liang Qingsong, Zhang Qingbao (Chinese language), July 17, 2015.

204 The Chinese term "jinhai fangyu" (近海防御)is sometimes translated in English as "near seas defense," rather than "offshore defense." ONI uses "offshore defense" as do official English-language documents of the Chinese government, such as the most recent defense white paper, "China's Military Strategy."

205 Annual Report to Congress; Military and Security Developments Involving the People's Republic of China 2017; Office of the Secretary of Defense; May 2017.

206 "China Naval Modernization: Implications for U.S. Navy Capabilities—Background and Issues for Congress," Congressional Research Service. November 18, 2005 -- December 13, 2017. URL: https://www.everycrsreport.com/reports/RL33153.html.

207 Office of Naval Intelligence; China's Navy 2007; Published 2007; p. 19.

208 Jane's, "China's AG600 amphibious aircraft makes maiden flight," January 04, 2018. URL: https://janes.intelink.ic.gov/docs/mags/jdw/jdw2018/fg_710922.htm.

209 "AG600 Seaplane Will Conduct Maiden Flight in China – May Become a Sharp Weapon to Protect Blue Sea Interests after Modifications," Sina, December 22, 2017, URL: http://slide.mil.news.sina.com.cn/h/slide_8_38692_59336.html#p=1.

210 "China's First Aircraft Carrier Could Be Named 'Liaoning' After Province," South China Morning Post Online (English language), September 11, 2012. URL: http://www.scmp.com/news/china/article/1033680/chinas-first-aircraft-carrier-could-be-named-liaoning-after-province.

211 "Defense Ministry Says China's First Aircraft Carrier Enters Service," Associate Foreign Press, September 25, 2012. URL: www.bbc.com/news/world-asia-china_19710040.

212 "Carrier To Firmly Safeguard Nation's Maritime Rights," Global Times Online in English, December 28, 2016. URL: http://www.globaltimes.cn/content/1026248.shtml.

213 "J-15 Fighter Jets From China's Liaoning Aircraft Carrier Make South China Sea Debut," South China Morning Post Online in English, January 3,2017. URL: http://www.scmp.com/news/china/diplomacy-defence/article/2058888/j-15-fighter-jets-chinas-liaoning-aircraft-carrier-make.

214 "Chinese aircraft carrier formation returns to Qingdao after Hong Kong Visit," The Straits Times, July 16, 2017, URL: http://www.straitstimes.com/asia/east-asia/chinese-aircraft-carrier-formation-returns-to-qingdao-after-hong-kong-visit.

215 "China launches first home-built aircraft carrier in latest display of growing naval power," South China Morning Post, April 26, 2017. URL: http://www.scmp.com/news/china/policies-politics/article/2090723/china-launches-first-home-built-aircraft-carrier-latest.

216 "J-15 Fighter Jets From China's Liaoning Aircraft Carrier Make South China Sea Debut," South China Morning Post Online in English, January 3, 2017. URL: http://www.scmp.com/news/china/diplomacy-defence/article/2058888/j-15-fighter-jets-chinas-liaoning-aircraft-carrier-make.

217 Dong, Winton, "China's Odyssey to Aircraft Carrier," Shenzhen Daily, May 9, 2017. URL: http://english.chinamil.com.cn/view/2017-05/09/content_7593538.htm.

218 Michael Martina, "China launches first home-built aircraft carrier amid South China Sea tension," Reuters, April 25 2017, https://www.reuters.com/article/us-china-military-carrier/china-launches-first-home-built-aircraft-carrier-amid-south-china-sea-tension-idUSKBN17S06B.

219 "The PLA Navy: New Capabilities and Missions for the 21st Century," 2015, Office of Naval Intelligence.

220 China's Military Strategy White Paper; The State Council Information Office of the People's Republic of China; May 2015, Beijing; http://news.xinhuanet.com/english/china/2015-05/26/c_134271001.htm.

221 "The PLA Navy: New Capabilities and Missions for the 21st Century," 2015, Office of Naval Intelligence.

222 "The PLA Navy: New Capabilities and Missions for the 21st Century," 2015, Office of Naval Intelligence.

223 Annual Report to Congress; Military and Security Developments Involving the People's Republic of China 2017; Office of the Secretary of Defense; May 2017.

224 Annual Report to Congress; Military and Security Developments Involving the People's Republic of China 2018; Office of the Secretary of Defense; 2018.

[225] Annual Report to Congress; Military and Security Developments Involving the People's Republic of China 2017; Office of the Secretary of Defense; May 2017.

[226] Annual Report to Congress; Military and Security Developments Involving the People's Republic of China 2017; Office of the Secretary of Defense; May 2017.

[227] James Bussert; China Builds Modern Marine Corps Force; April 2016; http://www.afcea.org/content/?q=china-builds-modern-marine-corps-force.

[228] China Country Handbook – 2008, Marine Corps Intelligence Activity, 2008.

[229] Cortez Cooper; PLA's "New Historic Missions:" Expanding Capabilities for a Re-emergent Maritime Power; June 2009; www.rand.org/pubs/testimonies/CT332.html.

[230] China's Military Strategy White Paper; The State Council Information Office of the People's Republic of China; May 2015, Beijing; http://news.xinhuanet.com/english/china/2015-05/26/c_134271001.htm.

[231] China's Military Strategy White Paper; The State Council Information Office of the People's Republic of China; May 2015, Beijing; http://news.xinhuanet.com/english/china/2015-05/26/c_134271001.htm.

[232] Li Faxin; The PLA Marines; China International Press; Published in 2013.

[233] Li Faxin; The PLA Marines; China International Press; Published in 2013.

[234] Li Faxin; The PLA Marines; China International Press; Published in 2013.

[235] Annual Report to Congress; Military and Security Developments Involving the People's Republic of China 2017; Office of the Secretary of Defense; May 2017.

[236] Blasko, Dennis. "What is Known and Unknown about Changes to the PLA's Ground Units," Jamestown Foundation, 11 May 2017.

[237] Annual Report to Congress; Military and Security Developments Involving the People's Republic of China 2017; Office of the Secretary of Defense; May 2017.

[238] Blasko, Dennis. "What is Known and Unknown about Changes to the PLA's Ground Units," Jamestown Foundation, 11 May 2017.

[239] Annual Report to Congress; Military and Security Developments Involving the People's Republic of China 2017; Office of the Secretary of Defense; May 2017.

[240] Li Faxin, The PLA Marines, China International Press; Published in 2013

[241] China's PLA Marines: An Emerging Force; www.the-diplomat.com; The Diplomat; 17 November 2013 and 19 November 2015.

[242] Global Security.org; July 2013 and November 2015; www.globalsecurity.org/military/world/plan-mc.html.

[243] Annual Report to Congress; Military and Security Developments Involving the People's Republic of China 2017; Office of the Secretary of Defense; May 2017.

[244] Office of Naval Intelligence; The PLA Navy: New Capabilities and Missions for the 21st Century; p. 17.

[245] Martin Andrew; ZBD05/ZLT05 Advanced Amphibious Assault Vehicles; Published September 2009; www.ausairpower.net/APA-PLA-AAV.html.

[246] Army-technology.com; ZBD-05 Amphibious Infantry Fighting Vehicle, China; www.army-technolog.com/projects/zbd-05-amphibious-infantry-fighting-vehicle.

[247] Li Faxin; The PLA Marines; China International Press; Published in 2013.

[248] Li Faxin; The PLA Marines; China International Press; Published in 2013.

[249] Annual Report to Congress; Military and Security Developments Involving the People's Republic of China 2018; Office of the Secretary of Defense; 2018.

[250] Mark R. Cozad, Nathan Beauchamp-Mustafaga, "People's Liberation Army Air Force Operations over Water: Maintaining Relvance in China's Changing Security Environment," RAND, 2017.

[251] Kevin Pollpeter and Kenneth Allen ed; 26 AUG 2015; DGI; The PLA as Organization: Reference Volume v2.0; pp 401.; http://www.andrewerickson.com/2015/12/a-classic-reference-with-renewed-relevance-download-the-pla-as-organization-v2-0/.

[252] Annual Report to Congress; Military and Security Developments Involving the People's Republic of China 2017; Office of the Secretary of Defense; May 2017.

[253] Franz-Stefan Gady, "Russia Starts Delivery of S-400 Missile Defense System to China;" The Diplomat; January 22, 2018. Accessed online 14 Feb 2018: https://thediplomat.com/2018/01/russia-starts-delivery-of-s-400-missile-defense-systems-to-china/Russia Starts Delivery of S-400 Missile Defense Systems to China.

[254] China Defence Today: PLA Reorganises Group Armies and Airborne Corps; 4 May 2017; p.1; https://sinodefence.com/2017/05/04/pla-reorganises-group-armies-and-airborne-corps.

[255] PLA Publication; Science of Army Operations; p. 171; June 2009.

[256] PLA Publication; Science of Army Operations; p. 171-172; June 2009.

[257] Annual Report to Congress; Military and Security Developments Involving the People's Republic of China 2017; Office of the Secretary of Defense; June 2017.

[258] Annual Report to Congress; Military and Security Developments Involving the People's Republic of China 2017; Office of the Secretary of Defense; May 2017.

[259] Annual Report to Congress; Military and Security Developments Involving the People's Republic of China 2017; Office of the Secretary of Defense; May 2017.

[260] Jamestown Foundation "The Strategic Support Force: China's Information Warfare Service" by John Costello; Feb 8, 2016; https://jamestown.org/program/the-strategic-support-force-chinas-information-warfare-service/.

[261] Annual Report to Congress; Military and Security Developments Involving the People's Republic of China 2017; Office of the Secretary of Defense; May 2017.

[262] "National Intelligence Law of the People's Republic of China," Xinhua, July 14 2017; URL: http://www.xinhuanet.com/politics/2017-06/28/c_1121222418.htm.

[263] "Chinese legislation points to new intelligence co-ordinating system", Jane's Intelligence Review, 5 Sept, 2017.

[264] "How China's Leader Is Building Team For Communist Party Congress," South China Morning Post Online (English language), August 7, 2017. URL: http://www.scmp.com/news/china/policies-politics/article/2104492/how-chinas-leader-building-team-communist-party.

[265] Annual Report to Congress: Military and Security Developments Involving the People's Republic of China 2016; Office of the Secretary of Defense, April 2016.

[266] "China and Northeast Asia." Jane's Sentinel Security Assessment, August 03, 2015.

[267] "Chinese Whispers – Chinese Intelligence Capabilities." Jane's Intelligence Review, July 03, 2013.

[268] John Costello, New America Foundation; 9 June 2016; "Chinese Intelligence Agencies: Reform and Future—Testimony before the U.S.-China Economic and Security Review Commission;" https://www.google.com/url?sa=t&rct=j&q=&esrc=s&source=web&cd=1&cad=rja&uact=8&ved=0ahUKEwifnbyJ-oLaAhUCTawKHY-DXCSwQFggpMAA&url=https%3A%2F%2Fwww.uscc.

gov%2Fsites%2Fdefault%2Ffiles%2FJohn%2520Costello_Written%2520Testimony060916.pdf&usg=AOv-Vaw2FvqV9y_gvL702OxRktAsa.

[269] Annual Report to Congress: Military and Security Developments Involving the People's Republic of China 2016; Office of the Secretary of Defense, April 2016.

[270] Mark Stokes and Russell Hsiao, "The People's Liberation Army General Political Department: Political Warfare with Chinese Characteristics," Project 2049 Institute, October 14, 2013. URL: http://project2049.net/publications.html.

[271] "China Observation Column: Xi Jinping's Promotion of PLA Young Turks," Tung Fang Jih Pao Online in Chinese, July 19, 2017, URL: orientaldaily.com.hk.

[272] Book, National Defense University Press; Mark A. Stokes; 2015; The People's Liberations Army and Contingency Planning in China; Ch. 6 Employment of National-Level PLA Assets in a Contingency: A Cross-Strait Conflict as Case Study. Pp 138-139; Compilation of paper writers out of a conference on "Contingency Planning, PLA Style".

[273] Joel Wuthnow and Phillip Saunders; Chinese Military Reform in the Age of Xi Jinping: Drivers, Challenges, and Implications; March 2017; Source is the Center for the Study of Chinese Military Affairs, Institute for National Strategic Studies, National Defense University.

[274] Peter Mattis, "China reorients strategic military intelligence," IHS Jane's Intelligence Review; 2017.

[275] Joel Wuthnow and Phillip Saunders; Chinese Military Reform in the Age of Xi Jinping: Drivers, Challenges, and Implications; March 2017; Source is the Center for the Study of Chinese Military Affairs, Institute for National Strategic Studies, National Defense University.

[276] Peter Mattis, "China reorients strategic military intelligence," IHS Jane's Intelligence Review; 2017.

[277] Joel Wuthnow and Phillip Saunders; Chinese Military Reform in the Age of Xi Jinping: Drivers, Challenges, and Implications; March 2017; Source is the Center for the Study of Chinese Military Affairs, Institute for National Strategic Studies, National Defense University.

[278] Peter Mattis, "China reorients strategic military intelligence," IHS Jane's Intelligence Review; 2017.

[279] Captain David A. Payne; Chinese Logistics Modernization; July-August 2008; www.alu.army.mil.

[280] IBT Pulse Newsletter; China's Military Researches Corruption Crackdown Helps, But The PLA's Problem is Bigger Than That; 2015; http://www.ibtimes.com.

281 Wendell Minnick; Report: China's Incomplete Transformation; 11 Feb 2015; http://www.defensenews.com.

282 CMC press conference on CMC organ reshuffle; http://eng.mod.gov.cn/TopNews/2016-01/12/content_4636291.htm.

283 Association for Asian Research; Chinese Military Logistics, The GLD System; 4 Nov 2004; http://www.asianresearch.org/articles/2354.html.

284 Zhang Tao, editor, "China established Joint Logistic Support Force," China Military Online, September 13, 2016, URL: http://eng.chinamil.com.cn/view/2016-09/13/content_7256651.htm.

285 China Military Online: Defense Ministry's News Conference on Joint Logistic Support System Reform; 14 SEP 2016; http://english.chinamil.com.cn/view/2016-09/14/content_7258622.htm.

286 China Military Online; 13 SEP 2016; China Establishes Joint Logistics Support Force; http://english.chinamil.com.cn/view/2016-09/13/content_7256651.htm.

287 Kevin McCauley; 15 February 2018; "China's Military Reforms and Modernization: Implications for the United States—Testimony before the U.S.-China Economic and Security Review Commission;" https://www.uscc.gov/Hearings/chinas-military-reforms-and-modernization-implications-united-states.

288 Sun Xingwei, Yan Shanpeng, "A Big Step in the Development of PLA's New Strategic Projection Force", Zhongguo Guofang Bao, August 15, 2017, URL: http://www.mod.gov.cn/mobilization/2017-08/15/content_4788860.htm.

289 Gao Zhiwen, "Civil-Military Integration Will Quickly Advance the Development of Strategic Projection Capability," Jiefangjun Bao, September 06, 2016, URL: http://www.81.cn/jfjbmap/content/2016-09/05/content_155683.htm.

290 China Politics and Policy; China Routes Rmb5tn Into Transport Infrastructure; https://www.ft.com/content/14926948-172b-11e6-b197-a4af20d5575e.

291 Development Research Center of the State Council of the People's Republic of China; Excerpt of Research On The Structure And Efficiency Of Traffic and Transportation Inter-cities in China; 23 Oct 2014; http://en.drc.gov.cn/2014-10/23/content_18792589.htm.

292 The Economist; The Flow Of Things; 12 July 2014; http://www.economist.com/news/china/21606899-export-superpower-china-suffers-surprisingly-inefficient-logistics-flow-things.

293 Armored Infantrymen Conduct Training in Frigid Environment; 15 FEB 2016; http://eng.chinamil.com.cn/news-channels/2016-02/15/content_6909279.htm.

294 Railway Technology; The World's 10 Longest Railway Networks; 2014; http://www.railway-technology.com/features/featurethe-worlds-longest-railway-networks-4180878.

295 China looks to the future with major highway; Oct 2011; World Highways; China Looks to the Future with Major Highway Plans; http://www.worldhighways.com/sections/world-reports/features/china-looks-to-the-future-with-major-highway-plans.

296 DHL; Logistics in China; https://www.dhl-discoverlogistics.com/cms/en/course/trends/asia/china.jsp.

297 Development Research Center of the State Council of the People's Republic of China; Excerpt of Research On The Structure And Efficiency Of Traffic and Transportation Inter-cities in China; 23 Oct 2014; http://en.drc.gov.cn/2014-10/23/content_18792589.htm.

298 China looks to the future with major highway; World Highways; China Looks to the Future with Major Highway Plans; Oct 2011; http://www.worldhighways.com/sections/world-reports/features/china-looks-to-the-future-with-major-highway-plans.

299 Global Times; China Passes New Law On National Defense Transport; 4 Sep 2016; http://www.globaltimes.cn/content/4466.shtml.

300 Huffington Post; Excerpt of Here's What You Need To Know About the South China Sea Disputes; 26 Feb 2016; www.huffingtonpost.com.

301 China Daily: China Spends 500 Mln Yuan to Support Public Private Partnerships; 5 Oct 2016; http://www.chinadailyasia.com/business/2016-10/05/content_15506276.html china spends US$75 to support PPP.

302 China Military Online: China Passes New Law on National Defense Transport; 3 Sep 2016; http://english.chinamil.com.cn/view/2016-09/03/content_7241207.htm.

303 China Military Online: China Passes New Law on National Defense Transport; 3 Sep 2016; http://english.chinamil.com.cn/view/2016-09/03/content_7241207.htm.

304 Weifeng Zhou; China Growing Assertiveness In The South China Sea; 11 May 2015; http://www.realinstitutoelcano.org/wps/portal/web/rielcano_en/contenido?WCM_GLOBAL_CONTEXT=/elcano/elcano_in/zonas_in/asia-pacific/ari60-2015-chinas-growing-assertiveness-in-the-south-china-sea.

305 The Straits Times; Chinese Firms Pump $20B Into Silk Road Projects; 24 Jun 2016; http://www.straittimes.com/asia/east-asia/chinese-firms-pump-20b-into-silk-road-projects.

306 Center for Security Studies in Security Policy, One Belt, One Road: China's Vision of Connectivity; Sep 2016; www.css.ethz.ch/en/center.

307 Puppet Masters; China's One Belt, One Road: The Dawn Of A New Eurasian Country; 4 Oct 2016; https://www.sott.net/article/330133-Chinas-One-Belt-One-Road-The-dawn-of-a-New-Eurasian-Century.

308 "Russia Delivers First S-400 Missile Defense Regiment to China," The Diplomat, April 3, 2018, URL: www.thediplomat.com/2018/04/russia-delivers-1st-s-400-missile-defense-regiment-to-china/; DOI 3 April 2018; Accessed 1 November 2018.

309 "China Confirms Deployment of New Light Tank," The Diplomat, October 12, 2017, URL: https://thediplomat.com/2017/06/china-confirms-deployment-of-new-light-tank/; Accessed 9 May 2018.

310 Annual Report to Congress: Military and Security Developments Involving the People's Republic of China 2017, Office of the Secretary of Defense, 2018.

311 "Pakistan Navy Fast Attack Craft (Missile Boat) Ceremony Held at Karachi Shipyard," Times of Islamabad Online in English, December 29, 2016. URL: https://timesofislamabad.com/29-Dec-2016/pakistan-navy-fast-attack-craft-missile-boat-ceremony-held-at-karchi-shipyard.

312 Qian Feng, "Sub Sales No Cause for Worry in India" Beijing Global Times Online, October 15, 2015. URL: http://www.globaltimes.cn/content/947437.shtml.

313 "Pakistan: PAF adds 16 more JF-17 Thunder jets," Islamabad The News Online in English, February 16, 2017. URL: https://www.thenews.com.pk/latest/186724-PAF-adds-16-more-JF-17-Thunder-jets.

314 Qian Feng, "Sub Sales No Cause for Worry in India" Beijing Global Times Online, October 15, 2015. URL: http://www.globaltimes.cn/content/947437.shtml.

315 "Pakistan: China to Supply Pakistan with Eight New Attack Submarines," The Express Tribune, Pakistan, August 31, 2016. URL: https://tribune.com.pk/story/1173324/china-supply-pakistan-eight-new-attack-submarines/.

316 "China: A Rising Drone Weapons Dealer to the World," CNBC, March 05, 2016, URL: http://www.cnbc.com/2016/03/03/china-a-rising-drone-weapons-dealer-to-the-world.html.

317 Government document, U.S. Department of State; Worldwide Military Expenditures and Arms Transfers 2017; Table III; https://www.state.gov/t/avc/rls/rpt/wmeat/2017/index.htm; Accessed 26 JUN 2018.

318 Government document, U.S. Department of State; Worldwide Military Expenditures and Arms Transfers 2016; Table III; https://www.state.gov/t/avc/rls/rpt/wmeat/2016/index.htm; Accessed 26 JUN 2018.

319 Government document, U.S. Department of State; Worldwide Military Expenditures and Arms Transfers 2015; Table III; https://www.state.gov/t/avc/rls/rpt/wmeat/2015/index.htm; Accessed 26 JUN 2018.

320 Government document, U.S. Department of State; Worldwide Military Expenditures and Arms Transfers 2014; Table III; https://www.state.gov/t/avc/rls/rpt/wmeat/2014/index.htm; Accessed 26 JUN 2018.

321 Government document, U.S. Department of State; Worldwide Military Expenditures and Arms Transfers 2013; Table III; https://www.state.gov/t/avc/rls/rpt/wmeat/2013/index.htm; Accessed 26 JUN 2018.

322 Government document, U.S. Department of State; Worldwide Military Expenditures and Arms Transfers 2012; Table III; https://www.state.gov/t/avc/rls/rpt/wmeat/2012/index.htm; Accessed 26 JUN 2018.

323 Government document, U.S. Department of State; Worldwide Military Expenditures and Arms Transfers 2005; Table III; https://www.state.gov/t/avc/rls/rpt/wmeat/2005/index.htm; Accessed 26 JUN 2018.

324 News Article, Jane's World Air Forces; 05 SEP 2017; Uzbekistan - Air Force; https://janes.intelink.ic.gov/docs/binder/jwaf/jwaf48/jwafa302.htm, Accessed 28 JUN 2018.

325 News Article, Jane's World Armies; 25 OCT 2017; Turkmenistan - Army; https://janes.intelink.ic.gov/docs/binder/jwar/jwar44/jwara254.htm, Accessed 28 JUN 2018.

326 News Article, Jane's World Armies; 01 JUN 2018; Belarus - Army; https://janes.intelink.ic.gov/docs/binder/jwar/jwar44/jwara113.htm, Accessed 28 JUN 2018.

327 News Article, Jane's World Armies; 06 APR 2018; Senegal - Army; https://janes.intelink.ic.gov/docs/binder/jwar/jwar44/jwara229.htm, Accessed 28 JUN 2018.

328 News Article, Jane's World Air Forces; 04 DEC 2017; Kazakhstan - Air Force; https://janes.intelink.ic.gov/docs/binder/jwaf/jwaf48/jwafa148.htm, Accessed 28 JUN 2018.

INTENTIONALLY LEFT BLANK

INTENTIONALLY LEFT BLANK

WWW.DIA.MIL

Made in the USA
Las Vegas, NV
05 June 2022